LITERATURE FROM CRESCENT MOON PU[

Sexing Hardy: Thomas Hardy and Feminism
by Margaret Elvy

Thomas Hardy's Jude the Obscure: A Critical Study
by Margaret Elvy

Thomas Hardy's Tess of the d'Urbervilles: A Critical Study
by Margaret Elvy

Stepping Forward: Essays, Lectures and Interviews
by Wolfgang Iser

Andrea Dworkin
by Jeremy Mark Robinson

German Romantic Poetry: Goethe, Novalis, Heine, Hölderlin
by Carol Appleby

Cavafy: Anatomy of a Soul
by Matt Crispin

Rilke: Space, Essence and Angels in the Poetry of Rainer Maria Rilke
by B.D. Barnacle

Rimbaud: Arthur Rimbaud and the Magic of Poetry
by Jeremy Mark Robinson

Shakespeare: Love, Poetry and Magic in Shakespeare's Sonnets and Plays
by B.D. Barnacle

Feminism and Shakespeare
by B.D. Barnacle

The Poetry of Landscape in Thomas Hardy
by Jeremy Mark Robinson

D.H. Lawrence: Infinite Sensual Violence
by M.K. Pace

D.H. Lawrence: Symbolic Landscapes
by Jane Foster

The Passion of D.H. Lawrence
by Jeremy Mark Robinson

Samuel Beckett Goes Into the Silence
by Jeremy Mark Robinson

*In the Dim Void: Samuel Beckett's Late Trilogy:
Company, Ill Seen, Ill Said and Worstward Ho*
by Gregory Johns

Andre Gide: Fiction and Fervour in the Novels
by Jeremy Mark Robinson

The Ecstasies of John Cowper Powys
by A.P. Seabright

Amorous Life: John Cowper Powys and the Manifestation of Affectivity
by H.W. Fawkner

Postmodern Powys: New Essays on John Cowper Powys
by Joe Boulter

Rethinking Powys: Critical Essays on John Cowper Powys
edited by Jeremy Mark Robinson

Thomas Hardy and John Cowper Powys: Wessex Revisited
by Jeremy Mark Robinson

Thomas Hardy: The Tragic Novels
by Tom Spenser

Julia Kristeva: Art, Love, Melancholy, Philosophy, Semiotics
by Kelly Ives

Luce Irigaray: Lips, Kissing, and the Politics of Sexual Difference
by Kelly Ives

Helene Cixous I Love You: The Jouissance of Writing
by Kelly Ives

Emily Dickinson: *Selected Poems*
selected and introduced by Miriam Chalk

Petrarch, Dante and the Troubadours: The Religion of Love and Poetry
by Cassidy Hughes

Dante: *Selections From the Vita Nuova*
translated by Thomas Okey

Friedrich Hölderlin: *Selected Poems*
translated by Michael Hamburger

Rainer Maria Rilke: *Selected Poems*
translated by Michael Hamburger

Walking In Cornwall
by Ursula Le Guin

Morning of Ecstasy

Selected Poems

Arthur Rimbaud

Translated and Introduced by Andrew Jary

CRESCENT MOON

First published 1994. Second edition 2007. Third edition 2012.
© Andrew Jary 1994, 2007, 2012.

Printed and bound in the U.S.A.
Set in Bodoni Book 10 on 14pt.
Designed by Radiance Graphics.

The right of Andrew Jary to be identified as the translator of *Morning of Ecstasy: Selected Poems* has been asserted generally in accordance with sections 77 and 78 of the Copyright, Designs and Patents Act 1988.

All rights reserved. No part of this book may be reprinted or reproduced, stored in a retrieval system, or transmitted, in any form or by any means, electronic, mechanical, photocopying, recording or otherwise, without permission from the publisher.

British Library Cataloguing in Publication data

Rimbaud, Arthur
Morning of Ecstasy: Selected Poems. – (European Poets Series)
I. Title II. Jary, Andrew III. Series
841.8

ISBN-13 9781861713650

CRESCENT MOON PUBLISHING
P.O. Box 1312, Maidstone
Kent, ME14 5XU
Great Britain
www.crmoon.com

Morning of Ecstasy:
Selected Poems

CONTENTS

A Note On Texts   15

POEMS

Les Poëtes de sept ans   18
Seven Year-Old Poets   19
Le bateau ivre   22
The Drunken Boat   23
Memoire   30
Memory   31
from Soleil et chair   34
from Sun and Flesh   35

from ILLUMINATIONS

Mystique   40
Mystic   41
Départ   42
Departure   43
from Barbare   44
from Barbarian   45
Aube   46
Dawn   47
from Solde   48

from Sale   49

from Angoisse   50

from Anguish   51

from Enfance   52

from Childhood   53

from Veillées   54

from Vigils   55

from Parade   54

from Circus   55

from Phrases   56

from Phrases   57

from Vies   58

from Lives   59

Génie   60

Genie   61

Matinée d'ivresse   64

Morning of Ecstasy   65

from UN SAISON D'ENFER

from Mauvais sang   68

from Bad Blood   69

from Déliries I: Vierge folle   72

from Delirium I: The Foolish Virgin   73

from L'Éclair   74

from Lightning   75

from Nuit de l'enfer   76

from Night in Hell   77

from L'Impossible   80

from The Impossible   81

from Matin   82

from Morning   83

from Adieu   84

from Farewell   85

from Déliries II: Alchimie du verbe   86
from Delirium II: Alchemy of the Word   87

      Illustrations   95
      A Note On Arthur Rimbaud   101
      Notes   109
      Bibliography   110

A NOTE ON TEXTS

The French text is taken from *Œuvres*, Gallimard, Paris, 1954.

ACKNOWLEDGEMENTS

To Gallimard, Paris, for the French text of Arthur Rimbaud's *Œuvres*, 1954.

All translations of Rimbaud's poetry are by the author, unless otherwise stated.

Morning of Ecstasy

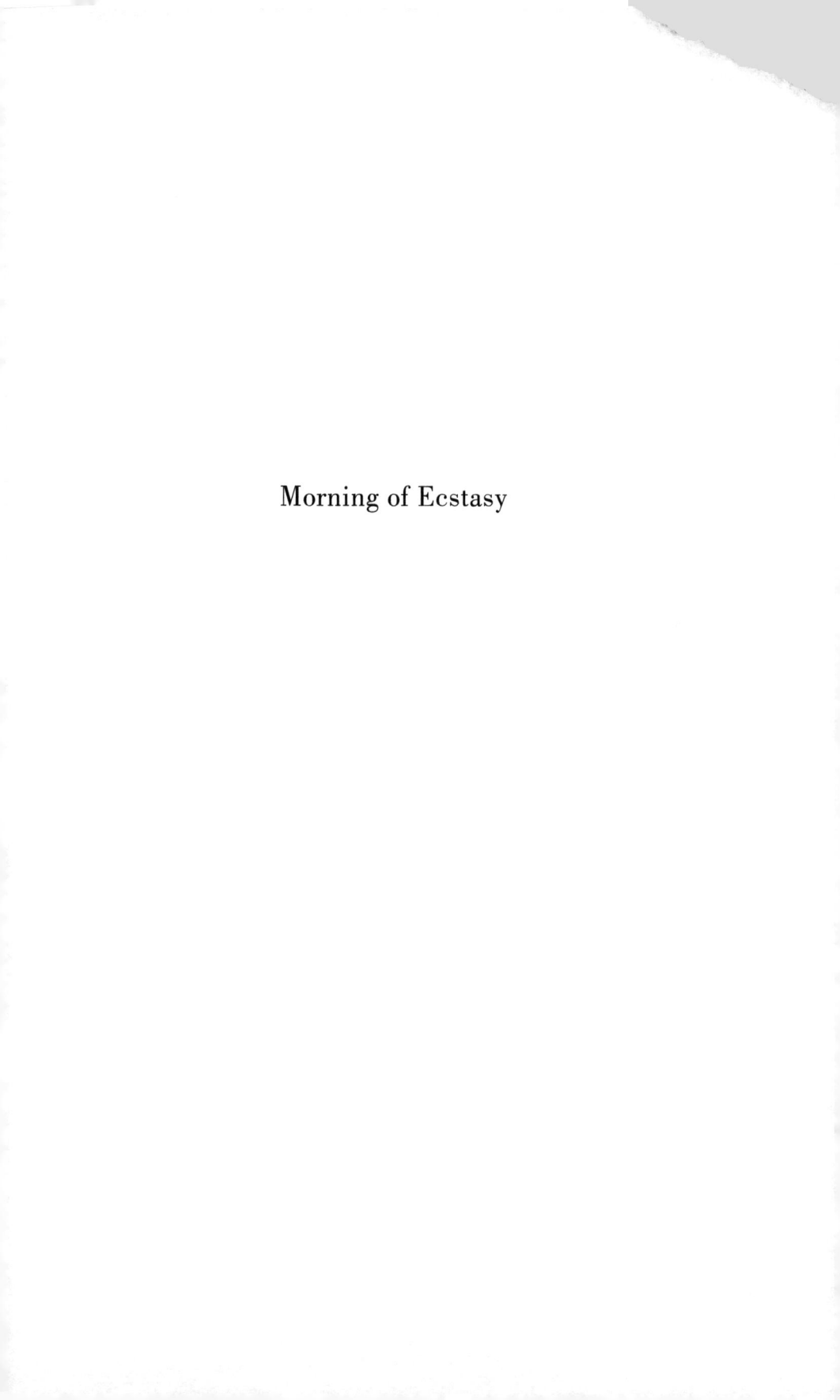

Arthur Rimbaud, from Henri Fantin-Latour's painting

Jef Rosman, Arthur Rimbaud, 1873 (above).
Pablo Picasso, Arthur Rimbaud (below).

LES POETES DE SEPT ANS

Et la Mère, fermant le livre du devoir,
S'en allait satisfaite et très fière sans voir
Dans les yeux bleus et sous le front plein d'éminences,
L'âme de son enfant livrée aux répugnances.

Tout le jour il suait d'obéissance; très
Intelligent; pourtant des tics noirs, quelques traits
Semblaient prouver en lui d'âcres hypocrisies!
Dans l'ombre des couloirs aux tentures moisies,
En passant il tirait la langue, les deux poings
A l'aine, et dans ses yeux fermés voyait des points.
Une porte s'ouvrait sur le soir: à la lampe
On le voyait, là-haut, qui râlait sur la rampe,
Sous un golfe de jour pendant du toit. L'été
Surtout, vaincu, stupide, il était entêté
À se renfermer dans la fraîcheur des latrines:
Il pensait là, tranquille et livrant ses narines.

Quand, lavé des odeurs du jour, le jardinet
Derrière la maison, en hiver, s'illunait,
Gisant au pied d'un mur, enterré dans la marne
Et pour des visions écrasant son œil darne,
Il écoutait grouiller les galeux espaliers.
Pitié! Ces enfants seuls étaient ses familers
Qui, chétifs, fronts nus, oiel déteignant sur la joue,
Cachant de maigres doigts jaunes et noirs de boue
Sous des habits puant le foire et tout vieillots,
Conversaient avec la douceur des idiots!
Et sui, l'ayant surpris à des pitiés immondes,
Sa mère s'effrayait; les tendresses, profondes,
De l'enfant se jetaient sur cet étonnement.
C'était bon. Elle avait le bleu regard, – qui ment!

SEVEN YEAR-OLD POETS

And the Mother, closing the workbook,
Went away all satisfied and very proud, without seeing,
In the blue eyes and under the forehead of bumps,
The soul of her child sunken in repugnancies.

All day he sweated obedience; very
Intelligent; but black tics, a few traits
Seemed to show in him bitter hypocrises!
In the shadow of the corridors with their moldy hangings,
He passed by, sticking out his tongue, with two fists
In his groin, and in his closed eyes he saw spots.
A door opened onto the evening; by the lamp
One saw him, up there, moaning on the stairs,
Under a flood of daylight falling from the roof. In summer
Especially, slow, stupid, he was determined
To lock himself in the coolness of the latrines:
He mused there, tranquil and opening his nostrils.

When, washed from the odours of the day, the small garden
Behind the house, in winter, was moonlit,
Lying at the foot of a wall, buried in soil,
And for visions rubbing his dazed eyes,
He heard the scruffy trees growing.
Pity! The only children who were his friends
Were those who, sickly, bare-headed, eyes running on their
                                        cheeks,
Hiding their thin yellow fingers, black with mud
Under old clothes stinking of fæces,
They talked with the softness of idiots!
And if she surprised him in these pitiful moments,
His mother was afraid; the profound tenderness
Of the child forced itself on her astonishment.
It was good. She had the blue-eyed look, – that lies.

A sept ans, il faisait des romans sur la vie
Du grand désert, où luit la Liberté ravie,
Forêts, soleils, rives, savanes! – Il s'aidait
De journaux illustrés où, rouge, il regardait
Des Espagnoles rire et des Italiannes.
Quand venait, l'oiel brun, folle, en robes d'indiennes,
– Huit ans, – la fille des ouvriers d'à côté,
La petite brutale, et qu'elle avait sauté,
Dans un coin, sur son dos, en secouant ses tresses,
Et qu'il était sous elle, il lui mordait les fesses,
Car elle ne portait jamais de pantalons;
– Et, par elle meurtri des poings et des talons,
Remportait les saveurs de sa peau dans sa chambre.

Il craignait les blafards dimanches de décembre,
Où, pommadé, su un guéridon d'acajou,
Il lisait une Bible à la tranche vert-chou;
Des rêves l'oppressaient chaque nuit dans l'alcôve.
Il n'aimait pas Dieu; mais les hommes, qu'au soir fauve,
Noirs, en blouse, il voyait rentrer dans le faubourg
Où les crieurs, en trois roulements de tambour,
Font autour des édits rire et gronder les foules.
– Il rêvait la praire amoureuse, où des houles
Lumineuses, parfums sains, pubescences d'or,
Font leur remuement calme et prennent leur essor!

Et comme il savourait surtout les sombres choses,
Quand, dans la chambre nue aux persiennes closes,
Haute et bleue, âcrement prise d'humidité,
Il lisait son roman sans cesse médité,
Plein de lourds ciels ocreux et de forêts noyés,
De fleurs de chair aux bois sidérals déployées,
Vertige, écroulements, déroutes et pitié!
– Tandis que se faisait la rumeur du quartier,
En bas, – seul, et couché sur des pièces de toile
Ecrue, et pressentant violemment la voile!

At seven years-old, he created novels of life
In the great desert, where exiled Liberty gleams,
Forests, suns, riverbanks, savannahs! – He was aided
By illustrated magazines where, red-faced, he saw
Spanish and Italian women laughing.
When she came, with brown eyes, wild, in calico clothes,
– Eight years-old, – the daughter of the workers next door,
The little brute, and when she jumped,
In a corner, on his back, pulling her tresses,
For she never wore knickers;
– And, beaten by her fists and heels,
He took back the taste of her skin to his room.

He loathed the grey Sundays of December
Where, his hair plastered, on a mahogany couch,
He read a bible with cabbage-green pages;
Dreams oppressed him each night in the alcove.
He did not like God; but the men, in the brown dusk,
Blackened, in jackets, he saw them returning to their homes,
Where town criers, with three drum rolls,
Made the crowds laugh and groan about edicts.
– He dreamt of a field of love, where luminous
Herds, with natural perfumes, puberties of gold,
Calmly moved, and then took flight!

And as he savoured dark things especially,
When, in his bare room with its closed shutters,
High and blue, with its arid humidity,
He read his novel, always thinking about it,
Full of heavy ochre skies and drowning forests,
Of flowers of flesh strewn in starry woods,
Vertigo, crumblings, disaster and pity!
– While the noise of the neighbourhood continued
Down below, – alone, and lying on pieces of
Canvas, and violently envisioning an unbleached sail.

LE BATEAU IVRE

Comme je descandais des Fleuves impassibles,
Je ne me sentis plus guidé par les haleurs:
Des Peaux-Rouges criards les avaient pris pour cibles,
Les ayant cloués nus aux poteaux de couleurs.

J'étais insoucieux de tous les équipages,
Porteur de blés flamands ou de cotons anglais.
Quand avec mes haleurs ont fini ces tapages,
Les Fleuves m'ont laissé descendre où je voulais.

Dans les clapotements furieux des marées,
Moi, l'autre hiver, plus sourd que les cerveaux d'enfants,
Je courus! Et les Péninsules démarrées
N'ont pas subi tohu-bohus plus triomphants.

La tempête a béni mes éveils maritimes.
Plus léger qu'un bouchon j'ai dansé sur les flots
Qu'on appelle rouleurs éternels de victimes,
Dix nuits, sans regretter l'œil niais des falots!

Plus douce qu'aux enfants la chair des pommes sures,
L'eau verte pénétra ma coque de sapin
Et des taches de vins bleus et des vomissures
Me lava, dispersant gouvernail et grappin.

Et dès lors, je me suis baigné dans le Poème
De la Mer, infusé d'astres, et lactescent,
Dévorant les azurs verts; où, flottaison blême
Et ravie, un noyé pensif parfois descend;

THE DRUNKEN BOAT

As I was moving down impassible rivers
I felt myself no longer guided by the haulers:
Howling indians had captured them for targets,
Nailing them nude to coloured stakes.

I was indifferent to all the crews,
Carrier of Flemish wheat or English cotton.
When with my haulers this uproar ceased,
The rivers let me drift where I wished.

In the furious splashing of the tides,
Me, the other winter, deafer than children's heads,
I ran! And the drifting peninsulas
Have not known a more triumphant hubbub.

The tempest blessed my ocean-going vigils,
Lighter than cork, I danced on the waves,
Which are called the eternal revolvers of victims,
Ten nights, without missing the silly eye of lighthouses!

Sweeter than children find the skin of hard apples,
The green water pierced my shell of pine
And spots of blue wine and vomit
Washed me, strewing rudder and hook.

And then, I bathed in the Poem
Of the Ocean, infused with stars, and milky,
Devouring the green azures; where, like flotsam pale
And raving, a pensive, drowned man sometimes sinks;

Où, teignant tout à coup les bleuités, délires
Et rhythmes lents sous les rutilements du jour,
Plus fortes que l'alcool, plus vastes que nos lyres,
Fermentent les rousseurs amìeres de l'amour!

Je sais les cieux crevant en éclairs, et les trombes
Et les ressacs et les courants: je sais le soir,
L'Aube exaltée ainsi qu'un peuple de colombes,
Et j'ai vu quelquefois ce que l'homme a cru voir!

J'ai vu le soleil bas, taché d'horreurs mystiques,
illuminant de longs figements violets,
Pareils à des acteurs de drames trés-antiques
Les flots roulant au loin leurs frissons de volets!

J'ai rêvé la nuit verte aux neiges éblouies,
Baiser montant aux yeux des mers avec lenteurs,
La circulation des sèves inouïes,
Et l'éveil jaune et bleu des phosphores chanteurs!

J'ai suivi, des mois pleins, pareille aux vacheries
Hystériques, la houle à l'assaut des récifs,
Sans songer que les pieds lumineux des Maries
Pussent forcer le mufle aux Océans poussifs!

J'ai heurté, savez-vous, d'incroyables Florides
Mêlant aux fleurs des yeux de panthéres à peaux
D'hommes! Des arcs-en-ciel tendus comme des brides
Sous l'horizon des mers, à de glauques troupeaux!

J'ai vu fermenter les marais énormes, nasses
Où pourrit dans les joncs tout un Léviathan!
Des écroulements d'eaux au milieu des bonaces,
Et les lointains vers les gouffres cataractant!

Where, suddenly, staining the blueness, delirium
And slow rhythms under the streaking sky,
Stronger than alcohol, vaster than our lyres,
The bitter redness of love seethes!

I know skies torn by lightning, and waterspouts,
And surf and currents; I know the night,
And sunrise exalted as a flight of doves,
And I've seen at times what man only thought he saw!

I have seen the low sun stained with mystic horrors,
Illuminated with long violet hazes,
Like actors in very ancient dramas,
The waves far off rolling their shivering of shutters!

I have dreamt of green nights with brilliant snow,
Kisses ascending slowly to the eyes of the sea,
The circulation of unknown juices,
And the awakening of the yellow and blue of singing
                                        phosphorous!

I have followed, during full months, the swell,
Like hysterical herds, attacking the reefs,
Without imagining that the luminous feet of Marys
Could muzzle the panting Oceans!

I have struck, you know, incredible Floridas,
Mixing flowers with the eyes of panthers and the skin
Of humans! Rainbows arched like bridle reins
Under the horizons of oceans, to greenish herds!

I have seen huge swamps ferment, nets
Where in the reeds a whole Leviathan rots!
Crumbling of water in the midst of calm,
And distances cataract towards the abyss!

Glaciers, soleils d'argent, flots nacreux, cieux de braises!
Echouages hideux au fond des golfes bruns
Où les serpents géants dévorés des punaises
Choient, des arbres tordus, avec de noirs parfums!

J'aurais voulu montrer aux enfants ces dorades
Du flot bleu, ces poissons d'or, ces poissoins chantants.
– Des écumes de fleurs ont bercé mes dérades
Et d'ineffables vents m'ont ailé par instants.

Parfois, martyr lassé des pôles et des zones,
La mer dont le sanglot faisait mon roulis doux
Montaint vers moi ses fleurs d'ombre aux ventouses jaunes
Et je restais, ainsi qu'une femme à genoux...

Presque ile, ballotant sur mes bords les querelles
Et les fients d'oiseux clabaudeurs aux yeux blonds.
Et je voguais, lorsqu'à travers mes liens fréles
Des noyés descendaient dormir, à reculons!...

Or moi, bateau perdu sous les cheveux des anses,
Jeté par l'ouragan dans l'éther sans oiseau,
Moi dont les Monitors et les voiliers des Hanses
N'auraient pas repêché la carcasse ivre d'eau;

Libre, fumant, monté de brumes violettes,
Moi qui trouais le ciel rougeoyant come un mur
Qui porte, confiture exquise aux bons poëtes,
Des lichens de soleil et des morves d'azur;

Qui courais, taché de lunules électriques,
Plance folle, escorté des hippocampes noirs,
Quand les juillets faisaient crouler à coups de triques
Les cieux ultramarins aux ardents entonnoirs;

Glaciers, suns of silver, pearly waves, fiery skies!
Hideous beaches at the end of brown gulfs,
Where giant serpents are devoured by insects
Falling, from twisted trees, with black perfumes!

I would've liked to have shown children those fishes
Of the blue wave, the fishes of gold, the singing fishes.
– Foam of flowers rocked my voyaging
And ineffable winds blew me at times.

Sometimes, a martyr tired of poles and zones,
The sea's sob created my gentle rolling,
Brought me shadowy flowers with yellow stalks
And I remained, like a kneeling woman…

Nearly an island, balancing on my sides the quarrels
And droppings of noisy, yellow-eyed birds.
And I voyaged on, and through my grail ropes
Drowned men sank to sleep, backwards!…

Now I, a lost boat under the foliage of caves,
Thrown by the tempest into the birdless æther,
All the monitors and Hansa merchant boats
Could not rescue my body drunk with the ocean;

Free, smoking, clothed in violet smog,
I who leapt through the reddening sky like a wall
And crying exquisite jam for good poets,
Lichens of sun and mucus of azures;

Who ran, speckled with little electric moons,
A mad plank, escorted by black seahorses,
When Julys battered with club-blows
The ultramarine skies with their burning funnels;

Moi qui tremblais, sentant geindre à cinquante lieues
Le rut des Béhémoths et les mælstroms épais,
Fileur éternel des immobilitiés bleues,
Je regrette l'Europe aux anciens parapets!

J'ai vu des archipels sidéraux! et des îles
Dont les cieux délirants sont ouverts au vogueur:
– Est-ce en ces nuits sans fonds que tu dors et t'exiles,
Million d'oiseaux d'or, ô future Vigeur? –

Mais, vrai, j'ai trop pleuré! Les Aubes sont navrantes.
Toute lune est atroce et tout soleil amer:
L'âcre amour m'a gonflé de torpeurs enivrantes.
O que ma quille éclate! O que j'aille à la mer!

Si je désire une eau d'Europe, c'est la flache
Noire et froide où vers le crépuscule embaumé
Un enfant accroupi plein de tristresses, lâche
Un bateau frêle comme un papillon de mai.

Je ne puis plus, baigné de vos langueurs, ô lames,
Enlever leur sillage aux porteurs de cotons,
Ni traverser l'orgueil des drapeaux et des flammes,
Ni nager sous les yeux horribles des pontons.

Me who trembles, sensing from fifty leagues
The rutting of Behemoths in heat and thick Mælstroms,
Eternal weaver of the blue immobilities,
I miss Europe with its ancient parapets!

I have seen starry archipelagos! and islands
Whose delirious skies are open to the voyager:
– Is it in these nights without end that you sleep and are exiled,
Million birds of gold, Oh future Vigour? –

But, in truth, I have cried too much! Dawns are heartbreaking.
Every moon is cruel and every sun is bitter:
Acrid love has swollen me with enervating torpor.
Oh let my keel break! Oh let me sink into the ocean!

If I desire a European shore, it is a pond
Black and cold where in the balming twilight
A stooping child full of sadness lets go
A boat frail as a May butterfly.

I can no longer, bathed in your languors, oh waves,
Follow in the wake of cotton tankers,
Nor traverse the pride of flags and flames,
Nor swim under the horrible eyes of prison ships.

MEMOIRE

I

L'eau claire; comme le sel des larmes d'enfance,
L'assaut au soleil des blancheurs des corps de femme;
la soie, en foule et de lys pur, des oriflames
sous les murs dont quelques pucelle eut la défense;

l'ébat des anges; – Non... le courant d'or en marche,
meut ses bras, noirs et lourds, et frais surtout, d'herbe. Elle
sombre, ayant le Ciel bleu pour ciel-de-lit, appelle
pour rideaux l'ombre de la colline et de l'arche.

II

Eh! l'humide carreau tend ses bouillons limpides!
L'eau meuble d'or pâle et sans fond les couches prêtes;
Les robes vertes et déteintes des fillettes
font les saules, d'où sautent les oiseaux sans brides.

Plus pure qu'un louis, jaune et chaude paupière
le souci d'eau – ta foi conjugale, ô l'Espouse! –
au midi prompt, de son terne miroir, jalouse
au ciel de chaleur la Sphère rose et chère.

III

Madame se tient trop debout dans la prairie
prochaine où neigent les fils du travail; l'ombrelle
aux doigts; foulant l'ombelle; trop fière pour elle;
des enfants lisant dans la verdure fleurie

leur livre de maroquin rouge! Hélas, Lui, comme
mille anges blancs qui se séparent sur la route,
s'éloigne par déla la montagne! Elle, toute

MEMORY

I

Clear water; like the salt of childhood tears,
the assault on the sun by the whiteness of women's bodies;
the silk, streaming, and of pure lily, flaming banners
under the walls once defended by a maid;

the play of angels; – No… the golden current flowing,
moves its arms, black and heavy, and especially cool, with grass. She,
dark, with the blue sky as a canopy, summons
for drapes the shadows of the hill and the arch.

II

Ah! the wet surface spreads its limpid broth!
The water fills the prepared beds with pale, depthless gold;
The green and faded clothes of the young women
are willows, from which birds leap unfettered.

Purer than a coin, a yellow and a warm eyelid
the marsh marigold – your conjugal faith, Oh Spouse! –
At noon prompt, from its lustreless mirror, vies
with the dear rosy Sphere in the sky grey with heat.

III

Madame stands too straight in the field
nearby where the filaments of work snow down; the parasol
in her fingers; stepping on the white flower; too proud for her;
the children in the flowering grass read

their book of red morocco! Alas, he, like
a thousand white angels scattering on the road,

froide, et noire, court! après le départ de l'homme!

IV

Regret des bras épais et jeunes d'herbe pure!
Or des lunes d'avril au cœur du saint lit! Joie
des chantiers riverains à l'abandon, en proie
aux soirs d'août qui faisent germer ces pourritures!

Qu'elle pleure à présent sous les remparts! l'haleine
des peupliers d'en haut est pour la seule brise.
Puis, c'est la nappe, sans reflets, sans source, grise:
un vieux, drageur, dans sa barque immobile, peine.

V

Jouet de cet œil d'eau morne, je n'y puis prendre,
ô canot immobile! oh! bras trop courts! ni l'une
ni l'autre fleur: ni la jaune qui m'importune,
là; ni la bleue, amie à l'eau couleur de cendre.

Ah! la poudre des saules qu'une aile secoue!
Les roses des roseaux dès longtemps dévorées!
Mon canot, toujours fixe; et sa chaîne tirée
Au fond de cet œil d'eau sans bords, – à quelle boue?

goes away over the mountain! She, all
cold, and dark, runs! after the departing man!

IV

Regret for the thick and young arms of pure grass!
Gold of April moons in the heart of the sacred bed! Joy
of abandoned boatyards, a prey
to August evenings which breed this rottenness.

Let her weep now, under the ramparts! the breath
of the poplars high above is the only breeze.
Then, this water, without reflections, without springs, grey:
an old man, a dredger, labours in his motionless barge.

V

Toy of this eye of sad water, I cannot reach anymore,
Oh motionless boat! oh! arms too short! not this
Nor the other flower: not the yellow one that bothers me,
there; nor the blue one, friend of the ash-coloured water.

Ah! the powder of the willows shaken by a wing!
The roses of the long-devoured reeds!
My boat, forever stationary, and its chain is caught
In the bottom of this boundless eye of water, – in what mud?

from SOLEIL ET CHAIR

Le Soleil, le foyer de tendresse et de vie,
Verse l'amour brûlant à la terre ravie,
Et, quand on est couché sur la vallée, on sent
Que la terre est nubile et déborde de sang;
Que son immense sein, soulevé par une âme,
Est d'amour comme Dieu, de chair comme la femme,
Et qu'il renferme, gros de séve et de rayons,
Le grand fourmillement de tous les embryons!

Et tout croît, et tout monte!

      – O Vénus, ô Déesse!

♣

S'il n'avait pas laissé l'imortelle Astarté
Qui jadis, émergeant dans l'immense clarté
Des flots bleus, fleur de chair que la vague parfume,
Montra son nombril rose où vint neiger l'écume,
Et fit chanter, Déesse aux grands yeux noirs vainqueurs,
Le rossignol aux bois et l'amour dans les cœurs!

Je crois en toi! je crois en toi! Divine mère,
Aphrodite marine! – Oh! la route est amère
Depuis que l'autre Dieu nous attelle à sa croix!
Chair, Marbe, Fleur, Vénus, c'est en toi que je crois!
♣
Tu viendras lui donner la Rédemption sainte!
– Splendide, radieuse, au sein des grandes mers
Tu surgiras, jetant sur le vaste Univers
L'Amour infini dans un infini sourire!

from SUN AND FLESH

The Sun, source of tenderness and life,
Pours burning love on the raving earth,
And, when one lies down in the valleys, one smells
How the earth is ripe and rich with blood;
How its immense bosom, raised by a soul,
Is of love, like God, of flesh like woman,
And it contains, big with juice and rays,
The huge swarming of all embryos!

And everything grows, and everything rises!

     – Oh Venus, Oh Goddess!

⚜

If only he [man] had not let go of immortal Astarte
Who once, emerging in the immense light
Of blue waves, flower of flesh by the wave perfumed,
Showed her rosy navel where the foam snows,
And made sing, goddess of great, black, conquering eyes,
The nightingales of the woods and love in hearts!

I believe in you! I believe in you! Divine mother,
Aphrodite of the ocean! – Oh! the way is hard;
Since the other God bound us to his cross;
Flesh, Marble, Flower, Venus, it is in you I believe!
⚜
You will come to give him saintly Redemption!
– Splendid, radiant, from the bosom of the great oceans
You will surge up, casting on the vast Universe
Infinite Love in its infinite smile!

Le Monde vibrera comme une immense lyre
Dans le frémissement d'un immense baiser!

– Le Monde a soif d'amour: tu viendras l'apaiser.

The world will vibrate like an enormous kiss!

– The World is thirsty for love; you will come to appease it.

from ILLUMINATIONS

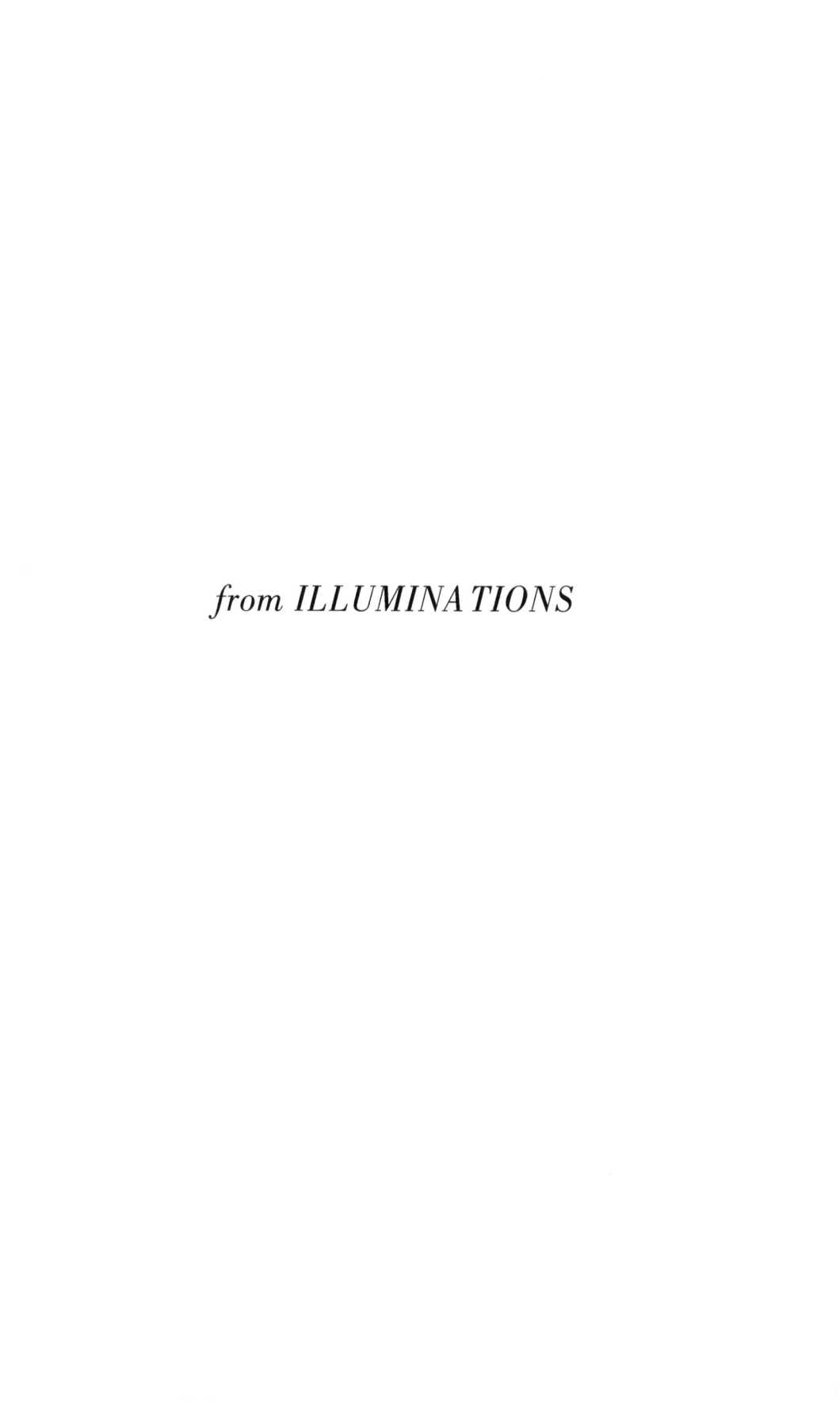

MYSTIQUE

Sur la pente du talus, les anges tournent leurs robes de laine dans les herbages d'acier et d'èmeraude.

Des prés de flames bondissent jusqu'au sommet du mamelon. A gauche le terreau de l'arête est piétiné par tous les homicides et toutes les batailles, et tous les bruit désastreux filent leur courbre. Derriére l'arête de droite la ligne des orients, des progrès.

Et, tandis que la bande en haunt du tableau est formée de la rumeur tournante et bondissante des conques des mers et des nuits humaines,

La douceur fleurie des étoiles et du ciel et du reste descend en face du talus, comme un panier, – contre notre face, et fait l'abîme fleurant et bleu là-dessus.

MYSTIC

On the side of the slope, the angels spin their woollen robes in the meadows of steel and emerald.

Fields of flame fly up to the top of the summit. To the left, the soil is trampled by all the murders and all the battles, and all the sounds of disaster turning in their curve. Behind the summit on the right is the line of the Orient, the progress.

And while the band of the top of the tableau is formed of the whirling rumour and leaping sounds of sea shells and human nights,

The flowery softness of the star and the sky and all the rest moves down opposite the slope, like a basket, – against our face, and makes the abyss below flowery and blue.

DÉPART

Assez vu. La vision s'est rencontrée à tous les airs.
　Assez eu. Rumeurs des villes, le soir, et au soleil, et toujours.
　Assez connu. Les arrêts de la vie. – O Rumeurs et Visions!
　Départ dans l'affection et le bruit neufs!

DEPARTURE

Seen enough. The vision meets itself in every air.

Had enough. Rumours of towns, in the evening, and in sunlight, and always.

Known enough. The halts of life. – Oh sounds and visions!

Departure into new affection and new sounds.

from BARBARE

Douceurs!
Les brasiers, pleuvant aux rafales de givre, – Douceurs! – les feux à la pluie du vent de diamants jetée par le cœur terrestre éternellement carbonisé pour nous. – O monde! –
(Loin des vieiless retraites et des vieilles flammes, qu'on entend, qu'on sent,)
Les brasiers et les écumes. La musique, virement des gouffres et choc des glaçons aux astres.
O Douceurs, ô monde, ô musique! Et là, les formes, les sueurs, les chevelures, et les yeux, flottant. Et les larmes blanches, bouillantes, – ô douceurs! – et la voix féminine arrivée au fond des volcans et des grottes arctiques.

from BARBARIAN

Happiness!

The braziers, frosty in the frosty winds, – Happiness! – the fire of the rain of the wind of diamonds thrown by the Earth's heat eternally burned for us. – Oh World! –

(Far from the old retreats and the old fires, which one hears, which one smells,)

The braziers and the foams. Music, turning of the gulfs and crashing of icicles with stars.

Oh Happiness, oh world, oh music! and there, forms, sweatings, hairs and eyes, floating. And the white tears, scalding, – oh happiness! and the feminine voice comes from inside volcanoes and arctic grottoes.

AUBE

J'ai embrassé l'aube d'été.

    Rien ne bougeait encore au front des palais. L'eau était morte. Les camps d'ombres ne quittaient pas la route du bois. J'ai marché, réveillant les haleines vives et tiédes, et les pierreries regardèrent, et les ailes se levèrent sans bruit.

    La première entreprise fut, dans le sentier déjà empli de frais et blêmes éclats, une fleur qui me dit son nom.

    Je ris au wasserfall blond qui s'échevela à travers les sapins: à la cime argentée je reconnus la déesse.

    Alors je levai un à un les voiles. Dans l'allée, en agitant les bras. Par la plaine, où je l'ai denoncée au coq. A la grand'ville, elle fuyait parmi les clochers et les dômes, et, courant comme un mendiant sur les quais de marbre, je la chassais.

    En haut de la route, près d'un bois de lauriers, je l'ai entourée avec ses voiles amassées, et j'ai senti un peu son immense corps. L'aube et l'enfant tombèrent au bas du bois.

    Au réveil il était midi.

DAWN

I have embraced the summer dawn.

Nothing budged yet in front of the palaces. The water was dead. Clusters of shadows would not leave the forest road. I walked, waking up the warm air and alive breath, and stones looked on, and wings rose up without a sound.

The first happening was, in the path already full of cool and white light, a flower which told me its name.

I laughed at the blond waterfall which cascaded wildly through the firs: at its silver summit I acknowledged the Goddess.

Then I lifted her veils, one by one. In the path, waving my arms. Through the meadow, where I denounced her to the rooster. In the big town, she fled between steeples and domes, and, running like a vagabond over the marble quays, I chased her.

Above the road, near a laurel grove, I cloaked her with her amassed veils, and I felt a little of her huge body. The dawn and the child fell at the edge of the grove.

On waking, it was noon.

from SOLDE

A vendre les applications de calcul et les sauts d'harmonie inouïs. Les trouvailles et les terms non soupçonnés, possession immédiate.

Elan insensé et infini aux splendeurs invisibles, aux délices insensibles, et ses secrets affolants pour chaque vice, et sa gaîté effrayante pour la foule.

from SALE

For sale applications of mathematics and obscure harmonic scales. Unknown discoveries and terms, possession immediate.

Wild and infinite leap to invisible splendours, to numbed delights, and the alluring secrets for each vice and fearful rejoicing for the crowds.

from ANGOISSE

Rouler aux blesseures, par l'air lasant et la mer; aux supplices, par le silence des eaux et de l'air meurtriers; aux tortures qui rient, dans leur silence atrocement houleux.

from ANGUISH

Roll me in wounds, through heavy air and the ocean; in pains, in the silence of waters and deadening air; in the tortures which laugh, in their silence of billowed atrocities.

from ENFANCE

Des fleurs magiques bourdonnaient. Les talus le berçaient. Des bêtes d'une élegance fabuleuse circulaient. Les nuées s'amassaient sur la haute mer faite d'une éternité de chaudes larmes.

from CHILDHOOD

Magic flowers were humming. The slopes were soothed. Beasts of a fabulous elegance circled about. Clouds amassing over the high seas made an eternity of warm tears.

from VEILLÉES

La plaque du foyer noir, de réels soleils des grèves: ah! puits des magies; seule vue d'aurore, cette fois.

from PARADE

J'ai seul la clef de cette parade sauvage.

from VIGILS

The plaque of the black earth, real suns of the shore: ah! well of magic; a solitary sight of the sunrise, this time.

from CIRCUS

I alone possess the key to this savage circus.

from PHRASES

Que j'aie réalisé tous vos souvenirs, – que je sois celle qui sait vous garrotter, – je vous étoufferai.

♣

Une matinée couverte, en juillet. Un goût de cendres vole dans l'air; – une odeur de bois suant dans l'âtre, – les fleurs rouies, – le saccage des promenades, – la bruine des canaux par les champs, pourquoi pas déjà les joujoux et l'encens?

J'ai tendu des cordes de clocher à clocher; des guirlandes de fenêtre à fenêtre; des chaînes d'or d'étoile à étoile, et je danse.

from PHRASES

When I have realized all our memories, – when I am the woman who can tie you up, – I will strangle you.

♣

A cloud-covered morning, in July. A taste of ashes floats in the air; an odour of wood sweating in the hearth, – ruined flowers, – the ravaging of paths, – drizzle on the canals by the fields, – why not now here toys and incense?

I have arched ropes from steeple to steeple; garlands from window to window; chains of gold from star to star, and I dance.

from VIES

Qu'est mon néant, auprès de la stupeur qui vous attend?

♣

Dans un vieux passage à Paris on m'a enseigné les sciences classiques. Dans une magnifique demeure cernée par l'Orient entier j'ai accompli mon immense œuvre et passé mon ilustre retraite. J'ai brassé mon sang.

from LIVES

What is my nothingness, compared to the stupor which awaits you?

♣

In an old alley in Paris I was taught the classic sciences. In a magnificent palace circled by the whole Orient, I completed my immense work and passed my illustrious retirement. I have drunk my own blood.

GÉNIE

Il est l'affection et le présent puisqu'il fait la maison ouverte à l'hiver écumeux et à la rumeur de l'été, lui qui a purifié les boissons et les aliments, lui qui est le charme des lieux fuyants et le délice surhumain des stations. Il est l'affection et l'avenir, la force et l'amour que nous, debout dans les rages et les ennuis, nous voyons passer dans le ciel de tempête et des drapeaux d'extase.

Il est l'amour, mesure parfaite et réinventé, raison merveilleuse et imprévue, et l'éternité: machine aimée des qualités fatales. Nous avons tous eu l'épouvante de sa concession et de la nôtre: ô jouissance de notre santé, élan de nos facultés, affection égoïste et passion pour lui, lui qui nous aime pour sa vie infinie...

Et nous nous le rappelons et il voyage... Et si l'Adoratin s'en va, sonne, sa promesse sonne: "Arrière ces superstitions, ces anciens corps, ces ménages et ces âges. C'est cette époque-ci qui a sombré!"

Il nes'en ira pas, il ne redescendra pas d'un ciel, il n'accomplira pas la rédemption des colères de femmes et des gaietés des homes et de tout ce peeche: car c'est fait, lui étant, et étant aimé.

O ses souffles, ses têtes, ses courses: la terrible célérité de la perfection des formes et de l'action.

O fécondité de l'esprit et immensité de l'univers!

Son corps! le dégagement rêvé, le brisement de la grâce croisée de violence nouvelle!

Sa vue, sa vue! tous les agenouillages anciens et les peines *relevés* à sa suite.

Son jour! l'abolition de toutes souffrances sonores et mouvantes dans la musique plus intense.

Son pas! les mitigations plus énormes que les anciennes invasions.

O Lui et nous! l'orgueil plus bienveillant que les charités perdues.

GENIE

He is affection and at present since he has opened the house to the froth of winter and the hum of summer, he who has purified drinks and foods, he who has the fascination of fleeting places and the superhuman delight of halts. He is affection and the future, the power and the love which we, upright in rages and boredoms, see pass by in the tempestuous sky and the drapes of ecstasy.

He is love, faultless and reinvented measure, unforeseen and wondrous reason, and eternity: machine loved for its fatal qualities. We have all known the horror of his concession and of ours: oh pleasure in our health, enthusiasm of our faculties, egoistical affection and passion for him, he who adores us for his infinite life...

And we, we recall him and he travels... And if Adoration moves, and tolls, his promise tolls: "Damn with these superstitions, these ancient bodies, these households and these ages. This is the epoch which has sunk!"

He will not leave, he will not sink down from the same sky, he will not accomplish the redemption of the anger of women and the joy of men and all this sin: for it is done, he is, and he is loved.

Of his breathing, his heads, his flights: the terrible swiftness of the perfection of forms and actions.

Oh fecundity of the spirit and the immensity of the universe!

His body! the dreamed-of release, the shattering of grace mixed with new violence!

His visions, his visions! all the ancient kneelings down and the punishments! *lifted* by his journey.

His day! the abolition of all echoing and restless sufferings in music more intense.

His pace! The migrations more enormous than ancient invasions.

Him and us! pride more benevolent than lost charities.

O monde! et le chant clair des malheurs nouveaux!

Il nous a connus tous et nous a tous aimés. Sachons, cette nuit d'hiver, de cap en cap, du pôle tumultueux au château, de la foule à la plage, de regards en regards, forces et sentiments las, le héler et le voir, et le renvoyer, et, sous les marées et au haut des déserts de neige, suivre ses vues, ses souffles, sons corps, son jour.

Oh world! and the clear song of new sorrows!

He knew all of us and loved us all. May we, this winter night, from cape to cape, from tumultuous pole to the castle, from the crowd to the beach, from glance to glance, power and feelings weary, hail him and see him, and return him, and, under tides and at the top of deserts of snow, follow his visions, his breathing, his body, his day.

MATINÉE D'IVRESSE

O *mon* Bien! O *mon* Beau! Fanfare atroce où je ne trébuche point! Chevalet féerique! Hourra pour l'œuvre inouïe et pour le corps merveilleux, pour la première fois! Cela commença sous les rires des enfants, cela finira par eux. Ce poison va rester dans toutes nos veines même quand, la fanfare tournant, nous serons rendu à l'ancienne inharmonie. O maintenant nous si digne de ces tortures! rassemblons fervemment cette promesse surhumaine faite à notre corps et à notre âme créés: cette promesse, cette démence! L'élégance, la science, la violence! On nous a promis d'enterrer dans l'ombre l'arbre du bien et du mal, de déporter les honnêtetés tyranniques, afin que nous amenions notre très pur amour. Cela commença par quelques dégouts et cela finit, – ne pouvant nous saisir sur-le-champ de cette éternité, – cela finit par une débande de parfums.

Rire des enfants, discrétion des esclaves, austérité des vierges, horreur des figures et des objets d'ici, sacrés soyez-vous parle souvenir de cette veille. Cela commençait par toute la rustrerie, voici que cela finit par des anges de flamme et de glace.

Petite veille d'ivresse, sainte! quand ce ne serait que pour le masque dont tu nous as gratifié. Nous t'affirmons, méthode! Nous n'oublions pas que tu as glorifié hier chacun de nos âges. Nous avons foi au poison. Nous savons donner notre vie tout entière tous les jours.

Voici le temps des ASSASSINS.

MORNING OF ECSTASY

Oh *my* Good! Oh *my* Beautiful! Atrocious fanfare where I do not stumble! Enchanted easel! Hurrah for the extraordinary work and for the wondrous body, for the first time! This began with the laughter of children, and it will end there. This poison will stay in all our veins even when, fanfare revolving, we return to the old discord. Oh now we are worthy of these tortures! let us fervently bring together again this superhuman promise made to our created bodies, our souls: this promise, this madness! Elegance, science, violence! they promised us they would bury in a shadow the tree of good and evil, and send away tyrannical honesty, so that we could bring forth our very pure love. It all began with some disgust and ended, – as we could not seize eternity on the spot – it ended with a rout of perfumes.

Laughter of children, discretion of slaves, austerity of virgins, horror of figures and objects from here, make sacred the memory of that night. It began in total loutishness, and here it ends with angels of fire and ice.

Little night of ecstasy, holy! if only for the mask you bequeathed to us. We affirm you, method! We will not forget that you glorified all our epochs yesterday. We have faith in poison. We will give our lives entirely every day.

This is the time of the ASSASSINS.

from UN SAISON EN ENFER

from MAUVAIS SANG

Les Gaulois étaient les écorcheurs de bêtes, les brûleurs d'herbes les plus ineptes de leur temps.

D'eux, j'ai: l'idolâtrie et l'amour du sacrilège; – oh! tous les vices, colère, luxure, – magnifique, la luxure; –surtout mensonge et paresse.

J'ai horreur de tous les métiers. Maîtres et ouvriers, tous paysans, ignobles. La main à plume vaut la main à charrue. – Quel siècle à mains! – Je n'aurai jamais ma main. Après, la domesticité mène trop loin.

♣

Ah! encore: je danse le sabbat dans une rouge clairière, avec des vieilles et des enfants.

♣

Qu'étais-je au siècle dernier: je ne me retrouve qu'aujourd'hui.

♣

C'est la vision des nombres. Nous allons à l'*Esprit*. C'est très certain, c'est oracle, ce que je dis. Je comprends, et ne sachant m'expliquer sans paroles païennes, je voudrais me taire.

♣

Me voici sur la plage armoricaine. Que les villes s'allument dans le soir. Ma journée est faite; je quitte l'Europe. L'air marin brûlera mes poumons; les climats perdus me tanneront. Nager, broyer l'herbe, chasser, fumer surtout; boire des liqueurs fortes comme du métal bouillant, – comme faisaient ces chers ancêtres autour des feux.

♣

Allons! La marche, le fardeau, le désert, l'ennui et la colère.

♣

– Ah! je suis tellement délaissé que j'offre à n'importe quelle divine image des élans vers la perfection.

O mon abnegation, ô ma charité merveilleuse! ici-bas, pourtant!

from BAD BLOOD

The Gauls were flayers of beasts, the most inept burners of herbs of their time.

From them I gain: idolatry and love of sacrilege; – oh! all the vices, anger, lust, – magnificent, this lust; above all lies and laziness.

I have a horror of all professions. Masters and workers, all are peasants, wretched. The hand holding the pen is no better than the hand holding the plough. –What an era of hands! – I will never keep my own hand. And then, domesticity leads me too far.

♣

Ah! again: I dance at the sabbath in a red clearing, with old women and children.

♣

What was I in the last era: I rediscover myself only today.

♣

It is the vision of numbers. We are moving towards *Spirit*. It is certain, this prophecy, I tell you. I understand and don't know how to explain it without using pagan words, I would rather keep quiet.

♣

Here I am on the beach of Brittany. Let cities light up in the night. My day is done; I leave Europe. The sea air will burn my lungs; lost climates will tan me. To swim, to pound the grass, to hunt, to smoke above all, to drink strong liquors like bubbling metal, – like the dear ancestors did around the fires.

♣

Let's go! The march, the burden, the desert, the lassitude, and anger.

♣

Ah! I am so easily abandoned that I offer to any divine image my feelings for perfection.

De profundis Domine, suis-je bête!

♣

Connais-je encore la nature? me connais-je? – *Plus de mots.* J'ensevelis les morts dans mon ventre. Cris, tambour, danse, danse, danse, danse! je ne vois même pas l'heure où, les blancs débarquant, je tomberai au néant.

Faim, soif, cris, danse, danse, danse, danse!

Oh my abnegation, oh my marvellous charity! down here, still!
De profundis Domine, I am an idiot!

♣

Do I know nature still? do I know myself? – No more words. I will bury the dead in my belly. Cries, drum, dance, dance, dance! I can't see the hour when, the whites disembarking, I will fall into nothingness.

Hunger, thirst, cries, dance, dance, dance, dance!

from DÉLIRES I: VIERGE FOLLE

Quelle vie! La vraie vie est absente. Nous ne sommes pas au monde.
♣
Je suis au plus profond de l'abîme, et je ne sais plus prier.

from DELIRIUM I: THE FOOLISH VIRGIN

What a life! Real life is absent. We are not in the world.

♣

I am in the deepest abyss, and I don't know how to pray anymore.

from L'ÉCLAIR

Non! non! à présent je me révolte contre la mort! Le travail parait trop léger à mon orgueil: ma trahison au monde serait un supplice trop court. Au dernier moment, j'attaquerais à droite, à gauche...

from LIGHTNING

No! no! now I rebel against death! Work seems too slight for my pride: my betrayal of the world would be too short a torture. At the last moment, I would attack to the right, to the left...

from NUIT DE L'ENFER

J'ai avalé une fameuse gorgée de poison. – Trois fois béni soit le conseil qui m'est arrivé! – Les entrailles me brûlent. La violence du venin tord mes membres, me rend difforme, me terrasse. Je meurs de soif, j'étouffe, je ne puis crier. C'est l'enfer, l'éternelle peine! Voyez comme le feu se relève! Je brûle comme il faut. Va, démon!

⚜

Et c'est encore la vie! – Si la damnation est éternelle! Un homme qui veut se mutiler est bien damné, n'est-ce pas? Je me crois en enfer, donc j'y suis. C'est l'exécution du catéchisme. Je suis esclave de mon baptême. Parents, vous avez fait mon malheur et vous avez fait le vôtre. Pauvre innocent! – L'enfer ne peut attaquer les païens. – C'est la vie encore! Plus tard, les délices de la damnation seront plus profondes. Un crime, vite, que je tombe au néant, de par la loi humaine.

⚜

La peau de ma tête se dessèche. Pitié! Seigneur, j'ai peur. J'ai soif, si soif! Ah! l'enfance, l'herbe, la pluie, le lac sur les pierres, *le clair de lune quand le clocher sonnait douze..* le diable est au clocher, à cette heure. Marie! Sainte Vierge!... – Horreur de ma bêtise.

⚜

Less hallucinations sont innombrables. C'est bien ce que j'ai toujours eu: plus de foi en l'histoire, l'oubli des principes. Je m'en tairai: poëtes et visionnaires seraient jaloux. Je suis mille fois le plus riche, soyons avare comme la mer.

Ah çà! l'horloge de la vie s'est arrêtée tout à l'heure. Je ne suis plus au monde. – La théologie est sérieuse, l'enfer est certainement *en bas* – et le ciel en haut. – Extase, cauchemar, sommeil dans un nid de flammes.

⚜

Je vais dévoiler tous les mystères: mystères religieux ou naturels, mort, naissance, avenir, passé, cosmogonie, néant. Je

from NIGHT IN HELL

I have swallowed a splendid mouthful of poison. – Three times blessed is the advice that came to me! – My entrails are burning me. The violence of the venom twists my limbs, deforms me, crushes me. I'm dying of thirst, I choke, I can't cry out. It is hell, eternal pain! See how the fire rises up! I burn as I should. Go, demon!

⚜

And this is still life! – If damnation is eternal! A man who mutilates himself is certainly damned, isn't he? I believe I am in hell, therefore I am. It is the work of catechism. I am enslaved by my baptism. Parents, you have made my unhappiness and you have made your own. Poor innocent! – Hell cannot attack pagans. – It is still life! Later, the delights of damnation will be more profound. A crime, quick, so I can fall into nothingness, by the law of humanity.

⚜

The skin on my head is drying up. Pity! Lord, I am scared. I am thirsty, so thirsty. Ah! childhood, grass, rain, the lake on the pebbles, *the moonlight when the bell tower sounds twelve..* the devil is in the bell tower, at this time. Mary! Holy Virgin!... – Horror at my idiocy.

⚜

The hallucinations are innumerable. This is what I've always had: no faith in history, forgetting principles. I will keep quiet: poets and visionaries would be jealous. I am a million times richer, so let's be avaricious as the sea.

Ah now! the clock of life stopped just this moment. I am no more in this world. – Theology is serious, Hell is certainly *down below* – and the sky's up high. – Ecstasy, nightmare, sleep in a nest of flames.

⚜

I will unveil all mysteries: religious mysteries or natural, death, birth, the future, the past, cosmogony, nothingness. I am sui maître en fantasmagories.

Ecoutez!...

J'ai tous les talents! – Il n'y a personne ici et il y a quelqu'un: je ne voudrais pas répandre mon trésor. – Veut-on des chants nègres, des danses de houris? Veut-on que je disparaisse, que je plonge à la recherche de l'*anneau*? Veut-on? Je ferai de l'or, des remèdes.

♣

Décidément, nous sommes hors du monde. Plus aucun son. Mon tact a disparu. Ah! mon château, ma Saxe, mon bois de saules. Les soirs, les matins, les nuits, les jours... Suis-je las!

Je devrais avoir mon enfer pour la colère, mon enfer pour l'orgueil, – et l'enfer de la caresse; un concert d'enfers.

master of phantasmagorias.

Listen!...

I have every talent! – There is nobody here and there is someone: I would not like to give out my treasure. – Would you like black songs, houri dances. Would you like me to disappear, to plunge to discover the *ring*. Would you? I will make gold, and remedies.

♣

Decidedly, we are out of the world. No more sound. My touch has gone. Ah! my castle, my Saxony, my willow woods. Evenings, mornings, nights, days... Am I tired!

I ought to have my hell for anger, my hell for pride, – and the hell of caresses, a concert of hells.

from L'IMPOSSIBLE

…Mes deux cents de raison sont finis! – L'esprit est autorité, il veut que je sois en Occident. Il faudrait le faire taire pour conclure comme je voulais.

J'envoyais au diable les palmes des martyrs, les rayons de l'art, l'orgueil des inventeurs, l'ardeur des pillards; je retournais à l'Orient et à la sagesse première et éternelle. – Il paraît que c'est un rêve de paresse grossière!

♣

Les philosophes: Le monde n'a pas d'âge. L'humanité se déplace, simplement. Vous êtes en Occident, mais libre d'habiter dans votre Orient, quelque ancien qu'il vous le faille, – et d'y habiter bien. Ne soyez pas un vaincu. Philosophes, vous êtes de votre Occident.

Mon esprit, prends garde. Pas de partis de salut violents. Exerce-toi!
– Ah! la science ne va pas assez vite pour nous!
– Mais je m'aperçois que mon esprit dort.

S'il était bien éveillé toujours à partir de ce moment, nous serions bientôt à la vérité, qui peut-etre, nous entoure avec ses anges pleurant!…

♣

O pureté! pureté!

C'est cette minute d'éveil qui m'a donné la vision de la pureté! – Par l'esprit on va à Dieu!

Déchirante infortune!

from THE IMPOSSIBLE

...My two cents of reason is ended! – The spirit is authority, it would like me to be in the Western world. It would have to be silenced if I can conclude as I wished.

I would send to the devil the palms of martyrs, the rays of art, the arrogance of inventors, the ardour of looters; I returned to the Orient and to the first and eternal wisdom. – It appears to be a dream of gross laziness!

♣

Philosophy: The world has no age. Humanity changes places, simply. You are in the West, but free to live in your Orient, which is as ancient as you like, – and to live there well. Do not be vanquished. Philosophers, you are of the West.

My spirit, be careful. Do not aim for violent salvation. Exercise yourself! – Ah! science cannot go fast enough for us! – But I see that my spirit sleeps.

If it were always fully awake from this moment onwards, we would soon reach the truth, which perhaps encircles us with its weeping angels!

♣

Oh purity! purity!

It is this moment of reawakening that has given me the vision of purity! – Through the spirit one goes to God!

What wrenching misfortune!

from MATIN

Moi, je ne puis pas plus m'éxpliquer que le mendiant avec ses continuels *Pater* et *Ave Maria*. *Je ne sais plus parler!*

Pourtant, aujourd-hui, je crois avoir fini la relation de mon enfer. C'était bien enfer; l'ancien, celui dont le fils de l'homme ouvrit les portes.

⚜

Quand irons-nous, par delà les grèves et les monts, saluer la naissance du travail nouveau, la sagesse nouvelle, la fuite des tyrans et des démons, la fin de la superstition, adorer – les premiers! – Noël sur la terre!

from MORNING

Me, I can no more explain myself than the beggar with his continual *Paters* and *Ave Marias*. *I don't know how to speak anymore!*

Still, today, I think I've finished the story of my hell. It was the real hell; the ancient place, whose gates were opened by the Son of Man.

♣

When will we go, over the shores and mountains, to salute the birth of the new work, the new wisdom, the flight of tyrants and demons, the end of superstition, to adore – the first ones! – Christmas on earth!

from ADIEU

L'automne déjà! – Mais pourquoi regretter un éternel soleil, si nous sommes engagés à la découverte de la clarté divine, – loin des gens qui meurent sur les saisons.

♣

– Quelquefois je vois au ciel des plages sans fin couvertes de blanches nations en joie. Un grand vaisseau d'or, au-dessus de moi, agite ses pavillons multicolores sous les brises du matin. J'ai créé toutes les fêtes, tous les triomphes, tous les drames. J'ai essayé d'inventer de nouvelles fleurs, de nouveaux astres, de nouvelles chairs, de nouvelles langues. J'ai cru acquérir des pouvoirs surnaturels. Eh bien! je dois enterrer mon imagination et mes souvenirs! une belle gloire d'artiste et de conteur emporté!

Moi! moi qui me suis dit mage ou ange, dispensé de toute morale, je suis rendu au sol, avec un devoir à chercher, et la réalit´rugueuse à étreindre! Paysan!

♣

Il faut être absolument moderne.

♣

Cependant c'est la veille. Recevons tous les influx de vigeur et de tendresse réelle. Et à l'aurore, armés d'une ardente patience, nous entrerons aux splendides villes.

from FAREWELL

Autumn already! But why regret an eternal sun, if we are engaged in the discovery of the divine light, – far from people who die with the seasons.

♣

Sometimes I see in the sky endless beaches covered with white nations rejoicing. A great ship of gold, above me, waves its multicoloured flags in the morning breeze. I have created all festivals, all triumphs, all dramas. I have tried to invent new flowers, new stars, new flesh, new languages. I believed I acquired supernatural powers. Now then I have to bury my imagination and my memories! A fine glory for an artist and a storyteller now ended!

Me! I who called myself a magician or angel, dispensing with all morality, I am sent back to the soil, with a duty to search, and drugged reality to embrace! Peasant!

♣

It's essential to be absolutely modern.

♣

Meanwhile this is the vigil. Let us receive all influx of vigour and real tenderness. And at dawn, armed with ardent patience, we will enter magnificent cities.

from DÉLIRES II : ALCHIMIE DU VERBE

A moi. L'histoire d'une de mes folies.

Depuis longtemps je me vantais de posséder tous les paysages possibles, et trouvais dérisoires les célébrités de la peinture et de la poésie moderne.

J'aimais les peintures idiotes, dessus de portes, décors, toiles de saltimbanques, enseignes, enluminures, populaires; la littérature démodée, latin d'église, livres érotiques sans orthographe, romans de nos aïeules, contes de fées, petits livres de l'enfance, opéras vieux, refrains niais, rhythmes naïfs.

Je rêvais croisades, voyages de découvertes dont on n'a pas de relations, républiques sans histoires, guerres de religion étouffées, révolutions de mœurs, déplacements de races et de continents: je croyais à tous les enchantements.

J'inventai la couleur des voyelles! – *A* noir, *E* blanc, *I* rouge, *O* bleu, *U* vert. – Je réglai la forme et le mouvement de chaque consonne, et, avec des rhythmes instinctifs, je me flattai d'inventer un verbe poétique accessible, un jour ou l'autre, à tous les sens. Je réservais la traduction.

Ce fut d'abord une étude. J'écrivais des silences, des nuits, je notais l'inexprimable. Je fixais des vertiges.

♣

La vieillerie poétique avait une bonne part dans mon alchimie du verbe.

Je m'habituai à l'hallucination simple: je voyais très franchement une mosquée à la place d'une usine, une école de tambours faite par les anges, des calèches sur les routes du ciel, un salon au fond d'un lac; les monstres, les mystères; un titre de vaudeville dressait des épouvantes devant moi.

Puis j'expliquai mes sophismes magiques avec l'hallucination des mots!

from DELIRIUM II :
ALCHEMY OF THE WORD

Now me. The story of one of my madnesses.

For a long time I bragged of possessing all possible landscapes, and I found stupid the celebrating of modern painting and poetry.

I liked idiot paintings, over doors, stage sets, backcloths for acrobats, signs, popular prints, old-fashioned literature, church latin, erotic books with misspellings, novels of our grandmothers, fairy tales, little children's books, old operas, foolish refrains, naïve rhythms.

I dreamt of crusades, voyages of discovery which were unrecorded, republics without histories, hushed-up religious wars, revolutions of customs, displacements of races and continents: I believed in all enchantments.

I invented the colour of vowels! – *A* black, *E* white, *I* red, *O* blue, *U* green. – I regulated the form and movement of each consonant, and, with instinctive rhythms, I flattered myself by inventing a poetic speech accessible, some day or other, to all the senses. I reserved translation rights.

It began as a study. I wrote silences, and nights, I noted the inexpressible. I fastened down vertigos.

♣

Poetic old-fashioned things formed a large part of my alchemy of the word.

I grew used to simple hallucination: I saw very clearly a mosque in place of a factory, a school of drummers made of angels, carriages on roads in the sky, a room at the bottom of a lake; monsters, mysteries; a vaudeville title drawn up with horrors in front of me.

Then I explained my magical sophisms with the hallucination of words!

Je finis par trouver sacré le désordre de mon esprit. J'étais oisif, en proie à une lourde fièvre: j'enviais la félicité des bêtes, – les chenilles, qui représentent l'innocence des limbes, les taupes, le sommeil de la virginité!

Mon caractère s'aigrissait. Je sais adieu au monde dans d'espèces de romances.

♣

J'aimai le désert, les vergers brûlés, les boutiques fanées, les boissons tiédies. Je me traînais dans les ruelles puantes et, les yeux fermés, je m'offrais au soleil, dieu de feu.

♣

Oh! le moucheron enivré à la pissotière de l'auberge, amoureux de la bourrache, et que dissout un rayon!

♣

Enfin, ô bonheur, ô raison, j'écartais du ciel l'azur, qui est du noir, et je vécus, étincelle d'or de la lumière *nature*, De joie, je prenais une expression bouffonne et égarée au possible.

Elle est retrouvée!
Quoi? l'éternité.
C'est la mer mêlée
   Au soleil.

Mon âme éternelle,
Observe ton vœu
Malgré la nuit seule
Et le jour en feu.

Donc tu te dégages
Des humains suffrages,
Des communs élans!
Tu voles selon...

– Jamais l'espérance,
Pas d'*orietur*.
Science et patience,
Le supplice est sûr.

I ended by finding sacred the chaos of my spirit. I was idle, a prey to a heavy fever: I envied the joy of beasts, caterpillars, who represented the innocence of limbo, moles, the sleep of virginity!

My character turned sour. I said farewell to the world in something like lovesongs.

✤

I loved the desert, burnt orchards, faded shops, tepid drinks. I dragged myself along foul-smelling alleys and, eyes closed, I offered myself to the sun, god of fire.

✤

Oh! the intoxicated gnat in the urinal of an inn, in love with weeds, and dissolved by a ray of light!

✤

Finally, oh happiness, oh reason, I cleared the sky of blue, which is black, sparkling of the gold of *nature's* light. In joy, I took on an expression clownish and distraught as possible:

It is rediscovered!
What? Eternity.
It's the sea frayed
   With the sun.

My eternal soul,
Observe your vow
In spite of the lonely night
And the day on fire.

So, free yourself
Of human suffrages,
Of common enthusiasms!
You fly depending on...

– Never hope,
No *orietur*.
Science and patience,
The torture is sure.

Plus de lendemain,
Braises de satin,
Votre ardeur
Est le devoir.

Elle est retrouvée!
– Quoi? – l'Eternité.
C'est la mer mêlée
   Au soleil

Je devins un opéra fabuleux: je vis que tous les êtres ont une fatalité de bonheur: l'action n'est pas la vie, mais une façon de gâcher quelque force, un énervement. La morale est la faiblesse de la cervelle.

A chaque être, plusieurs *autres* vies me semblaient dues. Ce monsieur ne sait ce qu'il fait: il est un ange. Cette famille est une nichée de chiens. Devant plusieurs hommes, je causai tout haut avec un moment d'une de leurs autres vies. – Ainsi, j'ai amié un porc.

Aucun des sophismes de la folie, – la folie qu'on enferme, – n'a été oublié par moi: je pourrais les redire tous, je tiens le système.

Ma santé fut mencée. La terreur venait. Je tombais dans des sommeils de plusieurs jours, et, levé, je continuais les rêves les plus tristes. J'étais mûr pour le trépas, et par une route de dangers ma faiblesse me menait aux confins du monde et de la Cimmérie, patrie de l'ombre et des tourbillons.

Je dus voyager, distraire les enchantments assemblés sur mon cerveau. Sur la mer, que j'aimais comme si elle eût dû me laver d'une souillure, je voyais se lever la croix consolatrice. J'avais été damné par l'arc-en-ciel. Le Bonheur était ma fatalité, mon remords, mon ver: ma vie serait toujours trop immense pour être dévouée à la force et à la beauté.

Le Bonheur! Sa dent, douce à la mort, m'avertissait au chant du coq, – *ad matutinum*, au *Christus venit*, – dans ls plus sombres villes:

O saisons, ô châteaux!
Quelle âme est sans défauts?

More in the morning,
Embers of satin,
Your ardour,
Is duty.

It is rediscovered!
– What? – Eternity.
It is the sea frayed
   With the sun.

I became a fabulous opera: I saw that all beings have a fatality of happiness: action is not for life, but a way of botching up some force, an enervation. Morality is the feebleness of the brain.

To everyone, several *other* lives seemed due to me. This gentleman doesn't know what he does: he is an angel. This family is a litter of dogs. In front of several men, I chatted loudly with a moment from one of their other lives. – That's how I loved a pig.

None of the sophisms of madness, – madness that is locked up, – was forgotten by men: I could repeat them all, I have the system.

My well-being was threatened. Terror came. I fell into a sleep of several days, and, rising, I continued having very sad dreams. I was ripe for death, and along a road of dangers my feebleness led me to the edges of the world and to Cimmeria, country of shadow and whirlwinds.

I had to travel, to divert the enchantments that crowded over my brain. On the sea, which I loved as if it were washing away a stain, I saw the consoling cross rise. I had been damned by the rainbow. Happiness was my misfortune, my remorse, my worm: my life would be always too huge to be devoted to strength and beauty.

Happiness! Its tooth, sweet as death, warned me of the song of the cockerel, – *ad matutinum,* at the *Christus venit,* – in the gloomiest cities:

   Oh seasons, oh castles!
   What soul is flawless?

J'ai fait la magique étude
Du bonheur, qu'aucun n'élude.

Salut à lui, chaque fois
Que chante le coq gaulois.

Ah! je n'aurai plus d'envie:
Il s'est chargé de ma vie.

Ce charme a pris âme et corps
Et dispersé les efforts.

  O saisons, ô châteaux!

L'heure de sa fuite, hélas!
Sera l'heure du trépas.

  O saisons, ô châteaux!

Cela s'est passé. Je sais aujord'hui saluer la beauté.

I have made the magic study
Of happiness, which no one eludes.

Salute to it, each time
The Gallic cock sings.

Ah! I will have no more desires:
It has taken over my life.

This charm has taken soul and body
And broken up my efforts.

    Oh seasons, oh castles!

The hour of its flight, alas!
It will be the hour of death.

    Oh seasons, oh castles!

That is gone. Today I know how to salute beauty.

ILLUSTRATIONS

Arthur Rimbaud

Arthur Rimbaud by his sister Isabelle (right), and at age twelve by Paterne Berrichon (below).

Henri Fantin-Latour, The Corner of the Table, 1872, Musée d'Orsay, Paris

Paul Verlaine by Eugène Carrière

ALCHEMY OF THE WORD

A NOTE ON ARTHUR RIMBAUD

Art makes life, gives life. For a time, when he was 16 or so, until he was 19, art was crucial for the psychic well-being of the ever-restless Arthur Rimbaud. Rimbaud (1854-1891) was the amazing poet who escaped from the utterly bland provincial town of Charleville in North France to wander the streets of Paris in poverty. After writing his *Illuminations* (1873-75) and *A Season in Hell* (1873), some of the most extraordinary poems of French – and world – literature, Rimbaud renounced it all for a hellish and profoundly boring life in Aden. 'Mortel, ange ET demon, autant dire Rimbaud,' as Rimbaud's lover, Paul Verlaine wrote ('Mortal, angel AND demon, that is to say Rimbaud'.)[1]

Arthur Rimbaud is the tornado of world poetry. He outblasts just about every other poet. For poets, he is more significant than the socalled 'founding fathers' or influential philosophers of the modern era: Karl Marx, Sigmund Freud, Friedrich Nietzsche and Albert Einstein. For other poets, he is 'everybody's favourite hippy', a Communard, a 'precursor of the current movement of subversion of Western notions of self, society, and discourse',[2] or the ultimate rebel, or a gay icon, or a savage mystic.[3]

Arthur Rimbaud is one of the most authentically rebellious of modern poets. Other poets have written of rebellion and radical action, but Rimbaud is one of the very few who actually carried it out. Picture the young poet in his mid-teens, utterly bored by the living deaths of suburban life, aching to run away to Paris. Though he was dragged back a number of times, Rimbaud's life after his early teens was never again centred in his homeland. True, he returned to his mother and family and homeland, but his true heartland, his landscape of the soul, was elsewhere. André Gide, one of Rimbaud's many followers (look at Gide's *Fruits of the Earth* or *Paludes*, for instance), wrote, famously: 'Familles, je vous haie' ('Families, I hate you'). Rimbaud did not personalize his hatred in the same way. It was not his family he hated, nor his background, nor his home ground. It was all manner of things, or nothing, or everything. he rebelled partly for the sake of rebellion. His early poetry is marked by an extraordinary virulence and anger. *Illuminations* and *A Season in Hell* his major works, are also powered by an immense anger – a cosmic anger, a psycho-cultural-spiritual turmoil.

Arthur Rimbaud's travels are incredibly energetic. Like D.H. Lawrence, Rimbaud simply would not keep still. He ran away in his teens to Paris and Brussels and had to be dragged back. He went to London twice. He travelled to Stuttgart, then walked to Würtenberg, then Switzerland, then Italy. From Italy he set off for the Cyclades, via Brindisi, then returned to Marseilles. He went to Scandinavia, Hamburg, Antwerp, and Rotterdam. With the Dutch army he landed in Java, then deserted it. In Vienna Rimbaud was expelled as a vagabond by the police. Passing St Helena in a ship that wouldn't stop there, he jumped overboard, but was brought back. Then there was Abyssinia and Aden, the horrific and mind-numbingly boring commercial exploits, before the final journey back to France, Rimbaud's own Calvary.

Arthur Rimbaud, it seems, was never satisfied. He seemed to be on the run all the time. His feet were always itching to be off. One recalls Rimbaud's famous poem 'Le Bateau ivre' (1871), that great, incandescent voyage, but also that exquisite moment of yearning at the end of Rimbaud's evocation of his provincial childhood, 'Le Poëtes de sept ans' (1871), where the poet rolls around on the canvas, dreaming of travel:

> Et comme il savourait surtout les sombres choses,
> Quand, dans la chambre nue aux persiennes closes,
> Haute et bleue, âcrement prise d'humidité,
> Il lisait son roman sans cesse médité,
> Plein de lourds ciels ocreux et de forêts noyés,
> De fleurs de chair aux bois sidérals déployées,
> Vertige, écroulements, déroutes et pitié!
> – Tandis que se faisait la rumeur du quartier,
> En bas, – seul, et couché sur des pièces de toile
> Ecrue, et pressentant violemment la voile!
>
> [And as he savoured dark things especially, when, in his bare room with its closed shutters, high and blue, with its arid humidity, he read his novel, always thinking about it, full of heavy ochre skies and drowning forests, of flowers of flesh strewn in starry woods, vertigo, crumblings, disaster and pity! – while the noise of the neighbourhood continued down below, – alone, and lying on pieces of canvas, and violently envisioning an unbleached sail.][4]

Arthur Rimbaud has been an inspiration for feminists as well as poets. American radical feminist Andrea Dworkin wrote:

> The books I loved when I was younger were by wild men: Dostoevsky, Rimbaud, Allen Ginsberg among the living, Baudelaire, Whitman, the undecorous. I read Freud and Darwin as great visionaries, their work culled from the fantastic, complex imagination.[5]

Andrea Dworkin is one of the few writers who came close to the fervour and idealism of the young Arthur Rimbaud; Dworkin writes:

> When young, I never thought about being homosexual or bisexual or heterosexual: only about being like Rimbaud. *Artiste* in the soon-to-be-dead mode was my sexual orientation, my gender identity, the most intense way of living: dying early the inevitable end of doing everything with absolute passion. (ib., 63)

For British poet Peter Redgrove, Arthur Rimbaud became his spiritual guide, his Virgil: 'Rimbaud escorted me many times through Hell and back again', writes Redgrove.[6]

> I used to read Rimbaud endlessly, and he saved me from terrible things when I was starting out after Cambridge. I had to do these office jobs, you see, which were not right, they're not right for anybody. I used to complete my office work in the mornings, and I would spend a long time in the pub at lunchtime reading Rimbaud, and seeing the world like this. Which gave me strength to continue.[7]

Arthur Rimbaud is, like Orpheus, always descending into Hell and returning. This is the basic journey of the shaman, the fragmentation and rebirth of the self. Rimbaud is constantly rebirthing himself, as the artist does, in each work. This 'descent and return' is a central experience in Rimbaud's world, chronicled in his extraordinary *A Season in Hell*, which describes a journey through hell and back again, a mythic journey which is linked to mythological figures such as Isis, Orpheus and Jesus.

Aged sixteen, Arthur Rimbaud wrote:

> the Poet makes himself a seer by a long and gigantic derangement of all the senses. All forms of love, suffering and madness. (*Complete Works* 307)

Arthur Rimbaud says a 'rational' derangement of the senses, meaning a systematic/ scientific deschooling, in the manner of the scientific approaches of the so-called 'Naturalist' novelists, such as Émile Zola and Gustave Flaubert. Rimbaud's experiment with himself, then, was a rigorous one, not just a dive into decadence and debauchery (although Rimbaud had plenty of that too). Further, Rimbaud had an ambiguous attitude to alcohol and drugs, and the 'Dionysian dance'[8] of his poetry is full of conflict, much of it unresolvable by art.[9]

One of the key aspects of Rimbaud's hallucinations is that they 'present the unreal as real', as Nathaniel Wing puts it.[10] This total immersion (immolation) in life, this diving into the flux or river of life, as Heraclitus put it, a grappling with Love and Strife, the twin poles of Empodecles' cosmological view, or, in the modern, post-Baudelairean/ post-de Sadean view, the poles of sex and death, the aim being so piquantly outlined by Rimbaud in his famous 'lettre du voyant' of May

15, 1871: 'All forms of love, suffering, and madness'.[11]

Peter Redgrove paraphrases Arthur Rimbaud thus:

> When Rimbaud said that what we must have to become seers is a reasoned disorder of the senses, he was talking so much about an upset or an explosion as a synæsthesia: the joining together of all the senses and their mutual illumination thereby. I think you could argue that synæsthesia was the central characteristic of poetry.[12]

Arthur Rimbaud speaks of a state of intoxication. There's no getting round it, there's no way of gentrifying Rimbaud's hallucinatory intoxication. It's madness Rimbaud speaks of, nothing less. And that's scary. It's scary for the individual because it alters everything, topples the known and the norms. Rimbaud's is a poetry of psychic and spiritual change that is firmly based in the body. An exclusively psychological transfiguration would not be enough for Rimbaud. He must involve the body. He must feel his own physical body going through the transformation. His derangement of the senses is precisely that, an *empirical* or *scientific* derangement or deschooling.

The senses. An emphasis on the senses occurs throughout Arthur Rimbaud's poetry. Cerebral his poetry is not, even though it is supremely 'intellectual' and scholarly in one way. Sure, Rimbaud's poetry is *poetry*, that is, a sophisticated cultural form of expression, which abides by many of the rules and norms of traditional art. Yes, but Rimbaud's poetry is also a poetry of wildness and derangement. He speaks of going mad, like many rock stars sing of going insane (Rimbaud has been eulogized by pop musicians such as Jim Morrison, Bob Dylan, Richard Hell and Patti Smith). Rimbaud's poetry is about being sensually, physically intoxicated. It's not drugs for drugs' sake. It's not art for art's sake, either. No. Rimbaud's theory of poetic intoxication is about a transformation of life itself, based in the body, the living body. Rimbaud's poetry speaks of feeling very alive, and wanting to achieve that state. It may seem that Rimbaud is not really talking about this goal at all in his poems, but in his letters he makes this point very clear. He lays into everything he loathes, everything that stands in his way. He clears the deck in his letters. He blasts his way through the time-worn edifices of the establishment.

Then comes Arthur Rimbaud's poetry, which is unquestionably magnificent. Such magnificence. This is why we keep returning to Rimbaud, because of this poetic munificence. The letters show Rimbaud explaining his poetic theories, but in the poems themselves he is not always so explicit. In the poetry, a variety of narrative voices contend for dominance. Ambiguity and confusion is natural in Rimbaud's way of intuitive poetry. In the poetry, Rimbaud moves back and forth, searching, describing, lambasting, praying, begging, desiring. It is a poetry of flux and impulses, a poetry which celebrates wildness and intoxication. There is no single 'masterplan' in the poetry – the letters provide that. There is, though, an incredible will to live, a will to live more, and deeper, and wilder, and more truthfully. That is, purely. Like many artists, Rimbaud is a disciple of purity, rather than 'truth', that is, 'truth' in the theological or philosophic sense. Rimbaud, like so many artists, wants to be true to himself. It was partly this failure to be self-pure, perhaps, that caused him to give up the poetic enterprise. Poetry failed him – because he asked too much of it. It couldn't deliver. It couldn't give Rimbaud the necessary whole body transformation, the transformation of body as well as soul – of bowels and loins, as D.H. Lawrence might say, as well as spirit and heart.

Arthur Rimbaud's experiential poetic technique was synæsthesia. That is, the multi-sensory intoxication of poetry, a poetry 'containing everything, smells, sounds, colours' (309). Rimbaud called it an 'alchemy of the word' and, in his amazing *A Season in Hell* he wrote:

> I liked idiot paintings, over doors, stage sets, backcloths for acrobats, signs, popular prints, old-fashioned literature, church latin, erotic books with misspellings, novels of our grandmothers, fairy tales, little children's books, old operas, foolish refrains, naïve rhythms. (Part II: *Alchemy of the Word*)

Arthur Rimbaud was so hungry for life. He had such a lust for life. He wanted to swallow everything. All at once, whole. Rimbaud founded his philosophy of poetry firmly on the individual. As Georges Poulet writes:

> For Rimbaud, to feel is to feel *oneself.* As sudden, even as violent, as certain physical contacts may be for him, they are always seen through a consciousness of self that never loses its lucidity.[13]

Arthur Rimbaud would gush, and often employ the dash – to connect different streams – of experience – which were coming at him – so fast – because of his mystical ecstasies – so the dash allows for the kind of flow appropriate for mysticism. Rimbaud also went for the prose poem, which also allowed for opening out in all directions. The two things, the 'religious' or synæsthetic experience and the prose poem, one of Rimbaud's innovations, go hand in hand in Rimbaud's poesie. The prose poem is the loose, open container for the synæsthesia, and the synæsthesia demands that sort of open treatment. In a similar fashion, those long, flowing stanzas of Rainer Maria Rilke's *Duino Elegies* were an integral part of that revelation which came upon Rilke so suddenly in 1912 – in the form of the 'terrifying Angel'.

Arthur Rimbaud's 'derangement of the senses', then, is a way of loosening the old ways and traditions and modes up. It is an opening-up, a relaxation into a new state, a going-through, a transformation, translation, transfiguration. Anaïs Nin spoke in one of her essays of loving words with the prefix *trans-*, *trans*-formation, *trans*-mutation, *trans*-portation. Going. Moving. Turning from one form to another. Motion. *Trans*mogrification. *Trans*cendence. A going-through, and beyond. But not the transcendence of the body, as in some forms of mysticism, such as Christianity or Sufism. Rimbaud wants to take the body with him in his transcendent, transformative experience. How terrible, then, for someone who lived so thrillingly and acutely in the body, for Rimbaud to waste away at age 36, to have his leg amputated. Rimbaud, who loved more than anything to walk, to roam wildly, to move across the globe following his desires, to have his leg cut away, to be bed-bound.

But Arthur Rimbaud's poetry has endured, and has enabled many devotees and readers to take flight. His poems, which he left behind as part of a former life which he no longer cared for, have had an extraordinary life of their own. Indeed, when people who are interested in what poetry can do and haven't read much b4 ask me which poet to read, I say Arthur Rimbaud above and beyond any other poet.

Beyond any other poet.

NOTES

1. P. Verlaine: "A Arthur Rimbaud I", *Dédicaces, Œuvres poétiques complètes* 1951, 431.
2. Edward J. Ahearn, 1985.
3. James Lawler, 219.
4. *Complete Works* 78, translation: author.
5. A. Dworkin: "Loving Books: Male/ Female/ Feminist" (1985), *Letters From a War Zone*, Secker & Warburg 1988.
6. P. Redgrove, "Rimbaud My Virgil", 172-178.
7. "Scientist of the Strange: An Interview with Peter Redgrove", Philip Fried, *Manhattan Review*, vol.3, no.1, Summer 1983.
8. Marcel Raymond: *Baudelaire au surréalisme*, Corti, Paris 1963.
9. Enid Rhodes Peschel, 1974.
10. Nathaniel Wing, 1974.
11. A. Rimbaud, 307. See Harold Bloom, 1988; Enid Starkie, 1973; Charles Chadwick, 1979.
12. Peter Redgrove: "The Science of the Subjective", *Poetry Review*, June 1987, 10.
13. Georges Poulet, 1984.

BIBLIOGRAPHY

BY ARTHUR RIMBAUD

Poèmes, ed. Pierre Moreau, Hachette 1963
Complete Works, Selected Letters, Wallace Fowlie, University of Chicago Press, Chicago 1966
Œuvres complètes ed. Antoine Adam, Gallimard, 1972
Poésies, Une saison en enfer, Illuminations ed. Louis Forestier, Gallimard, 1973
Illuminations, ed. Nick Osmond, Athlone Press 1976
Œuvres, ed. Suzanne Bernard & André Guyaux, Garnier, 1981
Illuminations, tr. Daniel Sloate, Guernica, Montreal 1990
A Season in Hell and Other Poems tr. Norman Cameron, Anvil, 1994
A Season In Hell, tr. Andrew Jary, Crescent Moon, 2007

ON ARTHUR RIMBAUD

Edward J. Ahearn: "Explosions of the Real: Rimbaud's Ecstatic and Political Subversions", *Stanford French Review*, 9, no. 1, Spring 1985
—. *Rimbaud, Visions and Habitations*, University of California Press 1983
—. "'Entends comme brame' and the Theme of Death in Nature in Rimbaud's Poetry", *French Review*, 43, 1970, 407-417
Charles Baudelaire: *Œuvres Complètes* Bibliothèque de la Pléiade, Gallimard, Paris 1975
Gwendolyn Bays: *The Orphic Vision: Seer Poets from Novalis to Rimbaud* University of Nebraska Press, Lincoln 1964
Suzanne Bernard: "Rimbaud et la création d'une nouvelle langue poétique", in *Le Poème en prose de Baudelaire jusqu'à nos jours*, Nizet 1959
Leo Bersani: *A Future For Astynanax*, Marion Boyars 1978
Harold Bloom, ed. *Arthur Rimbaud*, Chelsea House Publishers, New York 1988
C.H.L. Bodenham: "Rimbaud's *Poétique Sensationaliste* and Some 19th Century Medical Writing", *French Studies*, 38, no. 1, 1984, 32-40
Yves Bonnefoy: *Rimbaud par lui-même*, Seuil, 1961
Geoffrey Brereton: *An Introduction to the French Poets*, Methuen 1960

Peter Broome & Graham Chester: *The Appreciation of Modern French Poetry 1850-1950*, Cambridge University Press 1976
William Bryant: "Rimbaud, Disciple of Tristan L'Hermite?", *Romance Notes*, 22, no. 3, 1982
Charles Chadwick: *Etudes sur Rimbaud*, Nizet, 1960
—. *Rimbaud*, Athlone Press, 1979
R. Chisholm: *The Art of Rimbaud*, Melbourne University Press, Melbourne 1930
Robert Greer Cohn: *The Poetry of Rimbaud*, Princeton University Press, Princeton 1973
Henri de Bouillane de Lacoste: *Rimbaud et le problème des 'Illuminations'*, Mercure de France 1949
Yves Denis: "Glose 'un texte de Rimbaud: 'Après le déluge'", *Les Temps modernes*, 259, January, 1968
M. Eigeldinger: *La voyance avant Rimbaud*, Droz & Minard 1975
Shoshana Felman: "Arthur Rimbaud: Folie et modernité", in *La Folie et la chose littéraire*, Éditions du Seuil 1978
Angelika Felsch: *Arthur Rimbaud*, Bouvier, Bonn 1978
Wallace Fowlie: *Rimbaud's* Illuminations: *A Study in Angelism*, Harvill Press 1953
—. *Rimbaud*, University of Chicago Press, Chicago 1965
W.M. Frohock: *Rimbaud's Poetic Practice*, Harvard, Cambridge University Press, Mass., 1963
—. "Rimbaud's Poetics of Hallucination and Epiphany", *Romantic Review*, 46, no. 3, 1955
—. "Rimbaud amid Flowers", *MLN*, 76, no. 2, 1961
Harry Gilonis, ed. *Soleil et Chair: A Commemoration of the Centenary of Arthur Rimbaud*, Writers Forum 1991
Jean-Pierre Giusto: *Rimbaud créateur*, Presses Unversitaires de France 1980
—. "Rimbaud: 'Conte' et 'Royaute'", *Lez Valenciennes* 6, Winter 1981
—. "A Propos des *Illuminations*", *Revue d'histoire littérature de la France*, LXXVII, 1977
C.A. Hackett: *Rimbaud*, Hilary House, New York 1977
—. *Rimbaud l'enfant*, Corti 1948
—. "Rimbaud: *Illuminations* 'Aube'", in Nurse, 217-224
—. "Verlaine's Influence on Rimbaud", in Austin, 1961, 163-180
—. "Rimbaud and the 'Splendides villes'", *L'Esprit créateur*, 9, no. 1, Spring 1969
—. *Rimbaud: a critical introduction*, Cambridge University Press 1980
Phillip Herring: "Joyce and Rimbaud", in Suteit Badi Busrui & Bernard Benstock, eds. *James Joyce: An International Perspective*, Barnes & Noble, Otawa, New Jersey 1982
J.A. Hiddleton: "Rimbaud's 'Larme' and the *Gourde de colocasè*", *Romance Notes*, 23, no. 3, Spring 1983
John Porter Houston: *The Design of Rimbaud's Poetry*, Yale University Press, New Haven 1963
Frederic Jameson: "Rimbaud and the Special Text", in Tak-Wai Wong & M.A. Abbas, ed. *Rewriting Literary History*, Hong Kong University Press, Hong Kong 1984
Jordan Jones: "Renewing the Dance: René Daumal, the Surrealism of the Bardo, and Shamanic Poetry", *Heaven Bone*, no. 11, Spring 1994, 70-75

Atle Kittang: *Discours et jeu: essai d'analyse des textes d'Arthur Rimbaud,* University Press, Bergen & Grenoble 1975
K. Alfons Knauth: "Rimbaud's *Illuminations. Painted Plates* und Photostats *Images ou Tableaux de platte peinture*", *Poetica: Zeit-schrift für Sprach-und Literatur wissenschaft,* IX, 3-4, 1977
James Lawler: *Rimbaud's Theatre of the Self,* Harvard University Press, Cambridge, Mass., 1992
—. "Rimbaud as Rhetorician", in *The Language of French Symbolism*, Princeton University Press 1969
Roger Little: *Rimbaud: Illuminations*, Grant & Cutler 1983
—. "Rimbaud's 'Sonnet'", *Modern Language Review,* LXXV, 1980
—. "Rimbaud's 'Mystique': some observations", *French Stuies*, XXVI, 1972
—. "'H': l'énigme au-delà de l'énigme", *Revue es sciences humaines,* LVI, 184, October 1981
John Arthur MacCombie: *The Prince and the Genie: A Study of Rimbaud's Influence in Claudel,* University of Massachusetts Press, Amherst 1972
G.M. Mackling: "A Study of Beginnings and Ends in Arthur Rimbaud's *Illuminations*", *Neophilogus*, 68, no. 1, 1984
Henri Matarasso & Pierre Petitfils: *Album Rimbaud,* Gallimard 1967
—. *Vie de Rimbaud,* Hachette 1962
Andrew J. McKenna: "Lex Icon: Freud and Rimbaud", *Visible Language*, 14, no. 3, 1980
Lynda Donnelly McNeil: "Rimbaud: The Dialectical Play of Presence and Absence", *Boundary 2*, 12, no. 1, 1983
Henry Miller: *The Time of the Assassins: A Study of Rimbaud,* New Directions, New York 1956
E. Noulet: *Le Premier visage de Rimbaud,* Palais des Académies, Brussels 1953
Nick Osmond: "The Cheap Grey Notebook: An Authorized Sequence in Rimbaud's *Illuminations*", *19th Century French Studies,* 11, nos. 3-4, 1983
Marjorie Perloff: *The Poetics of Indeterminacy: Rimbaud to Cage,* Princeton University Press, Princeton 1981
Enid Rhodes Peschel: *Flux and Reflux: Ambivalence in the Poems of Arthur Rimbaud*, Libraire Droz, Geneva 1977
—. "Arthur Rimbaud: The Aesthetics of Intoxication", *Yale French Studies,* 50, 1974
Pierre Petitfils: *Rimbaud,* Julliard, 1982
Jacques Plessen: *Promenade et poésie: l'experience de la marche et du mouvement dans l'œuvre de Rimbaud,* Mouton, The Hague 1967
Georges Poulet: *Exploding Poetry/ Baudelaire/ Raimbaud*, tr. Françoise Meltzer, University of Chicago Press, Chicago 1984
Peter Redgrove: "Rimbaud My Virgil", *Sulfur* (30), Spring 1992, 172-178
A.R. Renéville: *Rimbaud le voyant*, La Colombe 1946
Revue de l'université de Bruxelles: Lectures de Rimbaud, nos 1-2, 1982
La Revue des lettres modernes, série Rimbaud, 1972-
Jean-Pierre Richard: "Rimbaud ou la poésie du devenir", in *Poésie et profondeur,* Seuil 1955
Renée Riese-Hubert: "The Use of Reversals in Rimbaud's *Illuminations*", *L'Esprit créateur*, 9, no. 1, 1969
Carol de Dobay Rifeli: "Rimbaud's 'À la musique': Language and Silence",

Romance Notes, 21, no. 2, 1980
Michael Riffaterre: "Sur la symphonique de l'obscurité en poésie: 'Promontoire' de Rimbaud", *French Review*, LV, 5, April, 1982
Jacques Rivière: *Rimbaud: dossier 1905-1925*, ed. Roger Lefèvre, Gallimard 1977
Marcel Ruff: *Rimbaud*, Hatier, 1968
Frederic St Aubryn: *Arthur Rimbaud*, Twayne, Boston 1975
Francis Scarfe: "A Stylistic Interpretation of Rimbaud", *Archivum Linguisticum*, 3, no. 2, 1951
Paul Schmidt: "Visions of Violence: Rimbaud and Verlaine", in Stambolian, 228-242
Michael Spencer: "A Fresh Look at Rimbaud's 'Métropolitain'", *Modern Language Review*, LXI, 1968
Enid Starkie: *Arthur Rimbaud*, Faber 1973
Kathleen Henderson Staudt: "The Text as Material and as Sign: Poetry and Incarnation in William Blake, Arthur Rimbaud and David Jones", *Modern Language Studies*, 14, no. 3, 1984
V.P. Underwood: *Rimbaud et l'Angleterre*, Nizet, 1976
Paul Verlaine: *Œuvres poétiques complètes*, ed. Y.-G. Le Dantec, Gallimard, 1951
Marie-Joséphine Whitaker: *La Structure du monde imaginaire de Rimbaud*, Nizet, 1972
Nathaniel Wing: *Present Appearances: Aspects of Poetic Structure in Rimbaud's 'Illuminations'*, Romance Monographs 1974
—. "The Autobiography of Rhetoric: On Reading Rimbaud's *Une Saison en enfer*", *French Forum*, 9, no. 1, 1984
—. "Metaphor and Ambiguity in Rimbaud's 'Memoire'", *Romantic Review*, 63, no. 3, 1972

WEBSITES

rimbaud-arthur.fr
mag4.net/Rimbaud

CRESCENT MOON PUBLISHING

ARTS, PAINTING, SCULPTURE

The Art of Andy Goldsworthy: Complete Works
Andy Goldsworthy: Touching Nature
Andy Goldsworthy in Close-Up
Andy Goldsworthy: Pocket Guide
Andy Goldsworthy In America
Land Art: A Complete Guide
The Art of Richard Long: Complete Works
Richard Long: Pocket Guide
Land Art In the UK
Land Art in Close-Up
Land Art In the U.S.A.
Land Art: Pocket Guide
Installation Art in Close-Up
Minimal Art and Artists In the 1960s and After
Colourfield Painting
Land Art DVD, TV documentary
Andy Goldsworthy DVD, TV documentary
The Erotic Object: Sexuality in Sculpture From Prehistory to the Present Day
Sex in Art: Pornography and Pleasure in Painting and Sculpture
Postwar Art
Sacred Gardens: The Garden in Myth, Religion and Art
Glorification: Religious Abstraction in Renaissance and 20th Century Art
Early Netherlandish Painting
Leonardo da Vinci
Piero della Francesca
Giovanni Bellini
Fra Angelico: Art and Religion in the Renaissance
Mark Rothko: The Art of Transcendence
Frank Stella: American Abstract Artist
Jasper Johns
Brice Marden
Alison Wilding: The Embrace of Sculpture
Vincent van Gogh: Visionary Landscapes
Eric Gill: Nuptials of God
Constantin Brancusi: Sculpting the Essence of Things
Max Beckmann
Caravaggio
Gustave Moreau
Egon Schiele: Sex and Death In Purple Stockings
Delizioso Fotografico Fervore: Works In Process 1
Sacro Cuore: Works In Process 2
The Light Eternal: J.M.W. Turner
The Madonna Glorified: Karen Arthurs

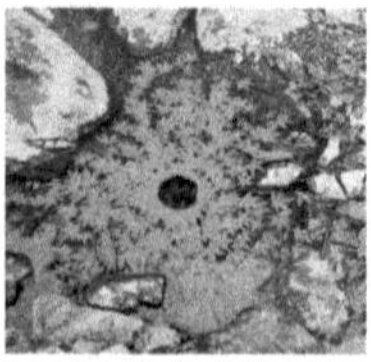

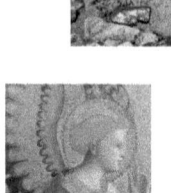

LITERATURE

J.R.R. Tolkien: The Books, The Films, The Whole Cultural Phenomenon
J.R.R. Tolkien: Pocket Guide
Tolkien's Heroic Quest
The *Earthsea* Books of Ursula Le Guin
Beauties, Beasts and Enchantment: Classic French Fairy Tales
German Popular Tales by the Brothers Grimm
Philip Ullman and *His Dark Materials*
Sexing Hardy: Thomas Hardy and Feminism
Thomas Hardy's *Tess of the d'Urbervilles*
Thomas Hardy's *Jude the Obscure*
Thomas Hardy: The Tragic Novels
Love and Tragedy: Thomas Hardy
The Poetry of Landscape in Hardy
Wessex Revisited: Thomas Hardy and John Cowper Powys
Wolfgang Iser: Essays and Interviews
Petrarch, Dante and the Troubadours
Maurice Sendak and the Art of Children's Book Illustration
Andrea Dworkin
Cixous, Irigaray, Kristeva: The *Jouissance* of French Feminism
Julia Kristeva: Art, Love, Melancholy, Philosophy, Semiotics and Psychoanalysis
Hélene Cixous I Love You: The *Jouissance* of Writing
Luce Irigaray: Lips, Kissing, and the Politics of Sexual Difference
Peter Redgrove: Here Comes the Flood
Peter Redgrove: Sex-Magic-Poetry-Cornwall
Lawrence Durrell: Between Love and Death, East and West
Love, Culture & Poetry: Lawrence Durrell
Cavafy: Anatomy of a Soul
German Romantic Poetry: Goethe, Novalis, Heine, Hölderlin
Feminism and Shakespeare
Shakespeare: Love, Poetry & Magic
The Passion of D.H. Lawrence
D.H. Lawrence: Symbolic Landscapes
D.H. Lawrence: Infinite Sensual Violence
Rimbaud: Arthur Rimbaud and the Magic of Poetry
The Ecstasies of John Cowper Powys
Sensualism and Mythology: The Wessex Novels of John Cowper Powys
Amorous Life: John Cowper Powys and the Manifestation of Affectivity (H.W. Fawkner)
Postmodern Powys: New Essays on John Cowper Powys (Joe Boulter)
Rethinking Powys: Critical Essays on John Cowper Powys
Paul Bowles & Bernardo Bertolucci
Rainer Maria Rilke
Joseph Conrad: *Heart of Darkness*
In the Dim Void: Samuel Beckett
Samuel Beckett Goes into the Silence
André Gide: Fiction and Fervour
Jackie Collins and the Blockbuster Novel
Blinded By Her Light: The Love-Poetry of Robert Graves
The Passion of Colours: Travels In Mediterranean Lands
Poetic Forms

POETRY

Ursula Le Guin: Walking In Cornwall
Peter Redgrove: Here Comes The Flood
Peter Redgrove: Sex-Magic-Poetry-Cornwall
Dante: Selections From the *Vita Nuova*  
Petrarch, Dante and the Troubadours
William Shakespeare: *The Sonnets*
William Shakespeare: Complete Poems
Blinded By Her Light: The Love-Poetry of Robert Graves
Emily Dickinson: Selected Poems
Emily Brontë: Poems
Thomas Hardy: Selected Poems 
Percy Bysshe Shelley: Poems
John Keats: Selected Poems
D.H. Lawrence: Selected Poems
Edmund Spenser: Poems
Edmund Spenser: *Amoretti* 
John Donne: Poems
Henry Vaughan: Poems
Sir Thomas Wyatt: Poems
Robert Herrick: Selected Poems
Rilke: Space, Essence and Angels in the Poetry of Rainer Maria Rilke
Rainer Maria Rilke: Selected Poems
Friedrich Hölderlin: Selected Poems
Arseny Tarkovsky: Selected Poems 
Novalis: *Hymns To the Night* 
Paul Verlaine: Selected Poems
Arthur Rimbaud: Selected Poems
Arthur Rimbaud: *A Season in Hell*
Arthur Rimbaud and the Magic of Poetry
D.J. Enright: By-Blows
Jeremy Reed: Brigitte's Blue Heart
Jeremy Reed: Claudia Schiffer's Red Shoes
Gorgeous Little Orpheus 
Radiance: New Poems
Crescent Moon Book of Nature Poetry
Crescent Moon Book of Love Poetry
Crescent Moon Book of Mystical Poetry
Crescent Moon Book of Elizabethan Love Poetry
Crescent Moon Book of Metaphysical Poetry
Crescent Moon Book of Romantic Poetry
Pagan America: New American Poetry

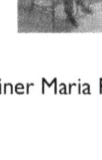

MEDIA, CINEMA, FEMINISM and CULTURAL STUDIES

J.R.R. Tolkien: The Books, The Films, The Whole Cultural Phenomenon
J.R.R. Tolkien: Pocket Guide
The *Lord of the Rings* Movies: Pocket Guide
The Cinema of Hayao Miyazaki
Hayao Miyazaki: *Princess Mononoke*: Pocket Movie Guide
Hayao Miyazaki: *Spirited Away*: Pocket Movie Guide
Tim Burton
Ken Russell
Ken Russell: *Tommy*: Pocket Movie Guide
The Ghost Dance: The Origins of Religion
The Peyote Cult
Cixous, Irigaray, Kristeva: The *Jouissance* of French Feminism
Julia Kristeva: Art, Love, Melancholy, Philosophy, Semiotics and Psychoanalysis
Luce Irigaray: Lips, Kissing, and the Politics of Sexual Difference
Hélene Cixous I Love You: The *Jouissance* of Writing
Andrea Dworkin
'Cosmo Woman': The World of Women's Magazines
Women in Pop Music
Discovering the Goddess (Geoffrey Ashe)
The Poetry of Cinema
The Sacred Cinema of Andrei Tarkovsky
Andrei Tarkovsky: Pocket Guide
Andrei Tarkovsky: *Mirror*: Pocket Movie Guide
Andrei Tarkovsky: *The Sacrifice*: Pocket Movie Guide
Walerian Borowczyk: Cinema of Erotic Dreams
Jean-Luc Godard: The Passion of Cinema
Jean-Luc Godard: *Hail Mary*: Pocket Movie Guide
Jean-Luc Godard: *Contempt*: Pocket Movie Guide
Jean-Luc Godard: *Pierrot le Fou*: Pocket Movie Guide
John Hughes and Eighties Cinema
Ferris Bueller's Day Off: Pocket Movie Guide
Jean-Luc Godard: Pocket Guide
The Cinema of Richard Linklater
Liv Tyler: Star In Ascendance
Blade Runner and the Films of Philip K. Dick
Paul Bowles and Bernardo Bertolucci
Media Hell: Radio, TV and the Press
An Open Letter to the BBC
Detonation Britain: Nuclear War in the UK
Feminism and Shakespeare
Wild Zones: Pornography, Art and Feminism
Sex in Art: Pornography and Pleasure in Painting and Sculpture
Sexing Hardy: Thomas Hardy and Feminism

In my view *The Light Eternal* is among the very best of all the material I read on Turner. (Douglas Graham, director of the Turner Museum, Denver, Colorado)

The Light Eternal is a model monograph, an exemplary job. The subject matter of the book is beautifully organised and dead on beam. (Lawrence Durrell)

It is amazing for me to see my work treated with such passion and respect. (Andrea Dworkin)

CRESCENT MOON PUBLISHING
P.O. Box 1312, Maidstone, Kent, ME14 5XU, Great Britain. www.crmoon.com

Lightning Source UK Ltd.
Milton Keynes UK
UKHW022033060720
366117UK00006B/1490